Constructing Knowledge Art:

An Experiential Perspective on Crafting Participatory Representations

Synthesis Lectures on Human-Centered Informatics

Editor
John M. Carroll, *Penn State University*

Human-Centered Informatics (HCI) is the intersection of the cultural, the social, the cognitive, and the aesthetic with computing and information technology. It encompasses a huge range of issues, theories, technologies, designs, tools, environments and human experiences in knowledge work, recreation and leisure activity, teaching and learning, and the potpourri of everyday life. The series will publish state-of-the-art syntheses, case studies, and tutorials in key areas. It will share the focus of leading international conferences in HCI.

2010

Constructing Knowledge Art: An Experiential Perspective on Crafting Participatory Representations
Al Selvin and Simon Buckingham Shum

ISBN: 978-3-031-01077-4   print
ISBN: 978-3-031-02205-0   ebook

DOI 10.1007/978-3-031-02205-0

A Publication in the Springer series
SYNTHESIS LECTURES ON HUMAN-CENTERED INFORMATICS #23
Series Editor: John M. Carroll, Penn State University

Series ISSN 1946-7680 Print   1946-7699 Electronic

Constructing Knowledge Art:

An Experiential Perspective on Crafting Participatory Representations

Al Selvin
Verizon Communications

Simon Buckingham Shum
University of Technology Sydney, Australia

SYNTHESIS LECTURES ON HUMAN-CENTERED INFORMATICS #23

ABSTRACT

This book is about how people (we refer to them as *practitioners*) can help guide participants in creating representations of issues or ideas, such as collaborative diagrams, especially in the context of Participatory Design (PD). At its best, such representations can reach a very high level of expressiveness and usefulness, an ideal we refer to as Knowledge Art. Achieving that level requires effective engagement, often aided by facilitators or other practitioners. Most PD research focuses on tools and methods, or on participant experience. The next source of advantage is to better illuminate the role of practitioners—the people working with participants, tools, and methods in service of a project's larger goals. Just like participants, practitioners experience challenges, interactions, and setbacks, and come up with creative ways to address them while maintaining their stance of service to participants and stakeholders. Our research interest is in understanding what moves and choices practitioners make that either help or hinder participants' engagement with representations. We present a theoretical framework that looks at these choices from the experiential perspectives of narrative, aesthetics, ethics, sensemaking and improvisation and apply it to five diverse case studies of actual practice.

KEYWORDS

participatory design, knowledge media, sensemaking, improvisation, reflective practice, aesthetics, ethics, narrative, facilitation, visualization, creativity, learning

Contents

Acknowledgments

We thank our close colleagues in this work over the years: Maarten Sierhuis, Jeff Conklin, Mark Aakhus, Michelle Bachler, Anna De Liddo, Clara Mancini, Alexandra Okada, Chuck Palus, and Ruth Deakin Crick. Special thanks to the reviewers for this volume: Ann Blandford, John Thomas, and Chuck Palus, whose comments made an enormous difference, and to Jack Carroll, Diane Cerra, and Deb Gabriel for their patient professionalism throughout this process. Finally, thanks to our KMI and OU colleagues for many years of collaborative sensemaking

CHAPTER 1

Introduction

I think the next century will be the century of complexity.

Stephen Hawking (Jan. 23, 2000, *San Jose Mercury News*)

As the complexity and interaction strengths in our networked world increase, man-made systems can become unstable, creating uncontrollable situations even when decision-makers are well-skilled, have all data and technology at their disposal, and do their best.

(Dirk Helbing, *Nature*, 2013)

As we navigate the second decade of the 21st century, humanity confronts the challenge of managing complexity at many scales, from the personal, to community, regional, national, and global. Finance, health, energy, education, urbanization, terrorism, etc. are the dilemmas we face that stretch us to the very limit of our cognitive and interpersonal capacities. The challenge, then, is to grow our collective capacity for sensemaking: to make sense of overwhelming amounts of data; to assess conflicting judgments about its trustworthiness; to resolve polarized interpretations about the implications; and to negotiate effective courses of action that all parties can commit to.

Better data and information/communication technologies (ICT) are not only drivers of these challenges, but also have key roles to play in managing them. However:

more data + more processing technology ≠ more insight or wisdom.

The nature of the problems we face means we will depend on nuanced human judgment over complex tradeoffs long into the foreseeable future because, despite their scientific and engineering foundations, these are not purely rational problems to be solved from first principles, using tried and tested algorithms or methods. The nature of policy formulation and implementation is fraught with the messiness of human life—social, organizational, political, and cultural dimensions cannot be simply wished away. Technically sound engineering blueprints are not sufficient when designing solutions to wicked problems, whose very definition is contested (Rittel and Webber, 1973; Conklin, 2005). Somehow, humanity's collective intelligence must chart courses through these white waters.

None of this is news, of course, and many people are working on these challenges. Under the broad heading of *collective intelligence* we see community activists, academics, businesses, and governments seeking to improve the social fabric of the internet in order to better harness the collective intelligence of human networks, operating largely asynchronously across time zones, augmented by machine intelligence.[1] Another strand of work (Bishop and Helbing, 2012) uses sensor networks, computational simulation of social systems, and complexity science to help us understand, increasingly in real time, the complex adaptive systems permeating society, whose structure and dynamics we are only beginning to grasp—often with tragic consequences when we consider our lack of control over financial markets or medical epidemics.

The work we will present in this book is what we will call Knowledge Cartography. Digital infrastructures generate huge quantities of data, rendered as higher-level visualizations of many sorts, around which many meetings (physical and virtual) will then be held to figure out what they mean.[2] Our focus is on a pervasive, critical, and hence surprisingly neglected piece of the collective intelligence jigsaw puzzle, namely: How *do we improve our capacity to create and use such representations?*

This focus on the dynamics of collective intelligence in small scale, synchronous contexts complements the social-semantic web/collective intelligence focus on large scale, asynchronous interaction. Knowledge Cartography also complements the big data and simulation efforts, shifting attention from machine-mining patterns in relatively low-level data to the highest levels of meaning-making that humans are capable of. Elsewhere we have argued for the need to add this critical layer of sensemaking to "big data" sensor networks and systems modeling (Buckingham Shum, et al. 2012). We need socio-technical infrastructures that recognize the role of humans in:

- weighing up complex tradeoffs—technical, interpersonal, financial, political, etc.;

- wrestling with ethical dilemmas;

- resolving conflicts between diverse stakeholders;

- crafting metaphorical power through stories; and

- empathizing by placing oneself in another's shoes.

This focus on cartography takes us back to humanity's most established mode of information diffusion and collective sensemaking: talking face to face, and inscribing marks in dirt, leaves, and clay. In the preface to *Knowledge Cartography* (Okada et al., 2008), we introduced mapping as follows.

> *Maps are one of the oldest forms of human communication. Map-making, like painting, pre-dates both number systems and written language. Primitive peoples made maps to orientate themselves in both the living environment and the spiritual worlds. Mapping enabled them to transcend the limitations of private, individual representations of terrain in order to augment group planning, reasoning and memory. Shared, visual representations opened new possibilities for focusing col-*

---

[1] Collective Intelligence for the Common Good: International Workshop, Sept. 29–30, 2014, The Open University UK. http://events.kmi.open.ac.uk/catalyst.

[2] One of the case studies in Chapter 4, the "Hab Crew" episode, is from such an effort.

lective attention, re-living the past, envisaging new scenarios, coordinating actions and making decisions.

Maps mediate the inner mental world and outer physical world. They help us make sense of the universe at different scales, from galaxies to DNA, and connect the abstract with the concrete by overlaying meanings onto that world, from astrological deities to signatures for diseases. They help us remember what is important, and explore possible configurations of the unknown.

Thus, our interest is in **how teams build new meaning using "representational artifacts,"** which take into account all the "hard" technical criteria as well as the "softer" human criteria mentioned above. In millions of meetings today, people will be scribbling and sketching on paper and whiteboards; typing lists of bullet points and outlines on screen; displaying, annotating and sharing photos, diagrams, maps, and websites. However, Knowledge Cartography is not about collaboration and visualization software per se (although much of our work has been with hypermedia visualization tools), but about **the human skillset needed to wield these and non-digital artifacts effectively, in real time, to engage participants and build new meaning in a group**. We've all been in meetings where a shared display added little value—but, we've all been in meetings when the right representation at the right moment helped to harness the collective energy and wisdom in the room, people connect with each other and the problem at a deeper level, and things move forward tangibly. At its best, such representations become highly evocative representations of designs, processes, and strategies, that serve not only as references, but also as touchstones of meaning, reflecting deep engagement and commitment by the participants who created them. Often the act of creation of the representation itself is as important as the value the representation may have to people viewing or using it later. We give the name "Knowledge Art" to that level of achievement. In the chapters that follow, our driving question will be: **How can practitioners help participants achieve this level in their representation-making?**

In his remarks at the Vannevar Bush Symposium at MIT on the 50th anniversary of "As We May Think," Doug Engelbart spoke about the need for evolution in understanding the role of human practitioners and new skillsets with sophisticated knowledge representation technology.

It's part of the thing of the easy to learn and natural to use thing that became sort of a god to follow and the marketplace is driving it and it's successful and you could market on that basis.... how do you ever migrate from a tricycle to a bicycle because a bicycle is very unnatural and very hard to learn compared to a tricycle, and yet in society it has superseded all the tricycles for people over five years old. So the whole idea of high-performance knowledge work is yet to come up and be in the domain. It's still the orientation of automating what you used to do instead of moving to a whole new domain in which you are going to obviously going to learn quite a few new skills. And so you make analogies of suppose you wanted to move up to the ski slopes and be mobile on skis. Well, just visiting them for an afternoon is not going to do it...

.... It's to externalize your thoughts in the concept structures that are meaningful outside and moving around flexibly and manipulating them and viewing them. It's a new way to operate on a new kind of externalized medium. So, to keep doing it in a model of the old media is just a hangup that someplace we're going to break that perspective and shift and then the idea of high performance and the idea of high performance teams who've learned to coordinate, to get that ball down the field together in all kinds of operations. I feel like the real breakthrough for us getting someplace is going to be when we say "All right, let's put together high-performance, knowledge-work teams and let's pick the roles they're going to play within our organizations in some way in such even though they operate very differently from their peers out in the rest of the organization they can interact with them and support them very effectively. So there are roles like that that would be very effective and everyone else can sort of see because they're interacting with these guys what they can do. And suppose it does take 200 hours of specialized training—that's less than boot camp.[3]

This book intends to contribute to this evolution. We describe the theoretical and practical motivation (Chapter 2) for **a language to describe the distinctive experience and skillset** that marks successful Knowledge Art (Chapter 3). To give you a feel for what's to come, in developing a language capable of expressing what we found when studying such practitioners, we found it necessary to draw from **Aesthetics** (how practitioners shape and craft the representation), **Ethics** (how a practitioner's actions affect other people), **Narrative** (meaning and causality applied to the flow of events), **Sensemaking** (the ways in which practitioners deal with situations of doubt or instability), and **Improvisation** (the spontaneous, creative moves that practitioners can make). This language has emerged in dialog with designing **ways of seeing this in action** (Chapter 4 and the Appendix). This lays the conceptual and empirical foundations for **future practitioner training and educational approaches** (Chapter 5).

To conclude, in an age of unprecedented complexity, we urgently need people who are fluent at "augmenting human intellect" with new kinds of "concept structures," to borrow Engelbart's iconic 1963 language. Our schools, universities, and workplaces train us to read and write as solo authors and speakers, paying little or no attention to the pervasive role of representations in our thinking with others. Understanding the experience and skillset that people fluent in such practice is a key first step. Perhaps this may come to be seen as a 21st century literacy—reading and writing symbolically in ways designed specifically to build real-time collective intelligence.

We hope this whets your appetite. If so, then let us take you on a journey...

---

[3] See http://www.dougengelbart.org/events/vannevar-bush-symposium.html.

CHAPTER 2

Participatory Design and Representational Practice

This book is about how people (we refer to them as *practitioners*) can help guide participants in creating representations of issues or ideas, such as collaborative diagrams. It's about the actions such people take that make a difference in how much, and how well, participants *engage* with the representations themselves. Sometimes there is close and thorough engagement, where people follow every move the practitioner is making, and call out what and how the practitioner should do (like "draw an arrow from that box to the other one!"), or even jump up and grab the marker (or mouse) and do it themselves. When a session is really humming, there is often such close engagement with the representation (see Figure 2.1).

Figure 2.1: An engaged participatory representational session. Everyone is focused on the representation as an integral part of the discussion.

Those sessions produce artifacts that are more truly reflective of participant interests and ideas than ones in which the participants sit back, or ignore, the representational work going on in the meeting. You've probably been in meetings where someone was creating some kind of diagram or process map on a whiteboard, and no one was paying much attention to what they were doing (see Figure 2.2).

Figure 2.2: A session where (as is often the case) participants are more engaged in talking with each or working on something else, while someone works on the ostensibly shared representation.

Our research interest is understanding what moves and choices practitioners make that either help or hinder participants' engagement with representations. In Chapter 3, we present a theoretical framework that looks at these choices from the perspectives of *narrative, aesthetics, ethics, sensemaking,* and *improvisation.* We're particularly interested in improvised moves because it's easiest to see what kinds of aesthetic and ethical choices practitioners make when rules and expected procedures are (even temporarily) abandoned. In this chapter, we explore what the research literature in Human-Computer Interaction (HCI) tells us about these phenomena.

In HCI, most discussion of participant interactions with facilitated representation-making falls into the domain of *Participatory Design* (PD) and similar methods, in which end users, or workers, or other people involved in a situation are brought into a design process. In the research literature for this field, there is much attention to various tools and techniques, and some to how PD projects should be planned and carried out, but very little attention to exactly what the facilitators (or practitioners) do in the individual meetings and sessions—especially not what happens when the meetings take unpredicted turns. From a research point of view, it is almost as if the sessions are thought to conduct themselves, with little need to understand the human role played by practitioners, and the ways the choices and moves they make in the heat of the moment make a difference to the sessions. We came to this line of inquiry after long involvement with creating participatory representations for design, strategy, and planning projects, including thousands of hours of facilitating such sessions. Often, participatory sessions experienced unexpected turns and facilitators had to improvise. We observed that the same occurs for nearly any PD-type facilitative method—at times, sensemaking moments arise, and practitioners improvise to get things back on track. These moments can have small or large impacts on the success of a particular session or an overall project. We want to understand the nature of these moments, the kinds of moves and choices practitioners make when they encounter them, and how to understand those moves within their context. By achieving a better understanding of what practitioners actually are faced with and learn to do in sessions, better ways of training and mentoring facilitative practitioners can be developed, akin to how musicians, architects, athletes, and others are coached. In turn, this will enhance the effectiveness of PD methods as well as other methods in which participatory engagement with visual, textual, aural, or other kinds of representations is central to an effort.

The intent of the book is to help reframe how we think about participatory practice, and particularly the role of the practitioner—how to lift understanding of that role from the instrumental, and get across something of its richness. Most PD research focuses on tools and methods, or on participant experience, all important perspectives. The next source of advantage is to better illuminate the role of practitioners—the people working with participants, tools, and methods in service of a project's larger goals. Just like participants, practitioners experience challenges, interactions, and setbacks, and come up with creative ways to address them while maintaining their stance of service to participants and stakeholders.

2.1   THE ROLE OF PRACTITIONERS

In this section, we focus on the role of facilitative practitioners in PD, especially on the ways in which aesthetic and ethical considerations play into their work with participants and representations.

Most PD studies treat practitioner concerns at a distance, if at all, or touch on them only at the level of project planning, selection of tools and techniques, or discussions of a project's functioning as a whole, rather than analyzing practitioner choices at the move-by-move level. Bergvall-Kåreborn and Ståhlbrost performed a review of all 15 articles in the 2006 Participatory Design conference, noting that only 3 of the 15 had "an ethical/political perspective on PD user participation" (2008: 104). Hecht and Maass (2008), as well as Lundberg and Arvola (2007), point out the paucity of PD studies examining practitioner moves and choices at the granular level. When they touch on practitioner issues at all, much research treats the practitioner as something of a cipher, an anonymous actor that chooses and applies tools and methods and organizes a project. Most more experiential accounts of PD projects focus more on participant reactions, uptake, and outcomes, rather than the role of practitioners.

Some PD researchers, however, do make practitioner ethics, facilitation, and reflective practice a major focus. Dearden and Rivzi (2008) discuss PD practitioners' interpersonal and facilitative skills, stressing the ethical dimensions of their role, such as the need to pay attention to power relationships in a project. They argue that listening and relationship-building need to be seen as core skills in PD, and that PD practitioners need to be reflective about their practice. Bergvall-Kåreborn and Ståhlbrost make distinctions between three main types of PD: "Design for users," "design with users," and "design by users," arguing that only the latter type treats designers as facilitators. They point out that none of the articles they review follows this type: "Within the information systems field taken broadly this is still a highly unusual approach" (2008: 106). More recently, Bratteteig and Wagner's (2014) PD workshop discusses power, participation, and the politics of PD projects.

Lundberg and Arvola (2007) evaluated the role of PD facilitation in card-sorting exercises, stressing the need to analyze the move-by-move level, and arguing that such facilitators need to move beyond "rote" interventions (such as reminding users to fill in the cards) with more "creative" moves. They discuss the ethical trade-offs inherent in deciding when to intervene as part of moving a design process along vs. allowing participants to pursue discussions that may not be part of the agenda (2007: 53). Hecht and Maass (2008) argue that PD facilitation needs to be a subject of direct research consideration. In their view, facilitators need to be trained in interactional and reflective practice techniques in order to make ethical choices. They claim that PD research that stays on the level of methods or tools is not enough, and that facilitating PD requires highly developed communication and interpersonal skills.

Bødker and Iversen argue that a "change of discourse" is needed in the PD field, which needs to be a "fully professional practice" requiring effective facilitation "in order to yield the full potentiality of user involvement." This can only come about through "ongoing reflection and off-loop reflection among practitioners" (2002: 11). Merkel et al. advocate that practitioners of community-based PD must reconceive their role "to avoid becoming yet another temporary resource taking on the role of the consultant who builds something, leaving behind a system that is difficult to use, fix, and modify" (2004: 2). Wagner and Piccoli argue that PD practitioners must change their orientation toward users and participants, especially learning to listen closely to participants during design sessions and adjusting expectations about the design accordingly, including their own (2007: 55).

Clark focuses on practitioner actions, involvement, and dilemmas in the context of PD project planning, stressing that practitioners need to be able to explain why participants and stakeholders will see value in methods and techniques that can appear "trivial, foreign, unnecessary, threatening and/or inefficient" (2008: 206). He provides excerpts from specific meetings as examples, looking at them through a performative lens (for example, as participants attempt to negotiate for project resources with governing boards). Similarly, Zeiliger et al. mention the issue of practitioner involvement from an ethical and interactional perspective, at the level of the whole project, in their description of pitfalls in PD projects (2008: 228).

Widening the lens to broader research in facilitative ethics, the idea that facilitator neutrality is a desirable, unproblematic, or sufficient concept has been widely critiqued. Aakhus argues that facilitation studies need to recognize intervention, not "objectivity," critiquing frameworks that de-emphasize the ethical "obligations and responsibilities" of facilitative practices, arguing that "objectivity" is an inaccurate way to frame practitioner actions (2003: 228). He calls for looking more deeply at how practitioner choices actively shape and affect participants, processes, and outcomes: "Facilitators need a discourse about practice that helps them articulate how they legitimately shape the direction, content, and outcome of meetings in the way they orchestrate interactions" (2001: 364). Jacobs and Aakhus (2002) focus on what Lovelace (2001) termed the "paradox of neutrality," a theme echoed in Bush and Folger's (1994) work on transformative mediation. These require that mediators recognize the limitations of operating from an ethical stance of neutrality, arguing that, intentionally or not, mediators make choices that emphasize or de-emphasize aspects of each disputant's "side" and ways of expressing, listening to, and acting on disputant utterances and emotions. Jacobs (2002) critiques neutrality in his examination of the styles and tactics used in mediation sessions. Benjamin (2001) states that "the mediator is not a remote, neutral, off-stage expert, but rather an active participant in the drama." For Stewart, "the facilitator cannot be neutral about the group's process, as both the facilitator and group discuss and reflect on the effectiveness of the processes being used" (2006: 423).

Cashtan's advocacy of "transparent facilitation" states that facilitators need a capacity of self-reflection, especially applicable during "charged moments" requiring extra "ethics" in a facilitative response (2005: 58). For Macfarlane, moral and ethical dilemmas are intrinsic to the mediator role and require personal judgment (2002: 56). Each decision to intervene lays open a universe of further choices. She argues that even apparently "functional" choices can have ethical consequences, and provides case studies of ethical choices on the move-by-move level, as do Bush and Folger (1994). Yoong (1999: 105) also argues for reflective practice as a primary training method for facilitators. For professional mediators, choice-making is constant as well as subjective: "The reality of mediation is that ethical judgment making occurs constantly, intuitively, and often unconsciously." (Macfarlane, 2002: 59). Macfarlane cites Cooks and Hale (1994) who draw connections between narrative, sensemaking, and ethics in their work on the construction of ethics in mediation. Yoong discusses the ethical dilemmas facilitators can find themselves in due to the multiple stakeholders they serve, for example in choosing between serving "management" (e.g., client) and participant goals: "a dual role that may [suffer] from competing actions" (Zorn and Rosenfeld, 1989: 98, cited in Yoong 1999: 102). Thomas calls for research on divergences between facilitators' espoused theories, and theories-in-use (actual behavior), particularly when the facilitator encounters challenging situations. In such circumstances, "the gap between an emerging facilitator's adopted, espoused theory and his or her theory-in-use could be problematic" (2008: 10).

2.1.1   AESTHETICS AND MEDIATING REPRESENTATIONS IN PD

Many PD researchers have discussed the ways that visual representations can bridge between end-users' and designers' perspectives in participatory design efforts (e.g., Greenbaum and Kyng, 1991; Blomberg and Henderson, 1990; Chin and Rosson, 1998; Muller, 1991). As we will discuss in more depth in the following chapter, any treatment of representations involves aesthetics—the giving of meaningful form via some medium. Although PD has been critiqued for ignoring or downplaying aesthetics (Bertelsen and Pold, 2004), some researchers do look at the importance of mediating representations in PD projects. For example, Hecht and Maass (2008) claim that such representations can play a central role, especially in teams with diverse kinds of participants: "Artifacts or representations that make sense to everybody facilitate cooperative work" (2008: 166). In their study of participatory mural creation at an interfaith conference, Tyler et al. (2005) describe how graphic facilitators used various means to encourage the participants to engage directly in decisions about what the representations should show (2005: 148). Iversen and Dindler advocate "tipping the scale towards transcendence" (2008: 138) by emphasizing the "aesthetic level" and skills of "aesthetic inquiry" in PD projects, requiring practitioners to attain familiarity with aesthetic concepts. Edmonds et al. (2006) discuss how practitioners created engagement with interactive artworks by constructing a participatory research studio at a museum, where the public could interact with artists in the process of refining the interactive objects.

Despite these considerations, most accounts of PD practice leave such practice concerns, dilemmas, and experiential aspects in the background. Little work examines PD facilitation at the move-by-move level or provides close analysis of the interactions of participants and practitioners with representations. Many PD researchers have called for increased emphasis on PD facilitation as a professional practice, requiring reflective and experiential approaches, as we'll explore in more depth in the following chapter. It is here we propose that Knowledge Art, as a normative ideal, gives us a unique viewpoint by which to understand and evaluate instances of participatory representational practice. Rather than treating such practice as the rational application of tools and methods, we look at it as the attempt of people to create meaningful representations of the ways they have connected ideas together. The experience of doing this in groups is better treated from an experiential than a techno-rational perspective. At its best, such practice can result in highly evocative representations of designs, processes, and strategies, that serve not only as references, but also as touchstones of meaning. We use that ideal as a way to look at instances of practice and see where they do, or don't, rise to that level of meaning and integration.

2.2   SUMMARY

In this chapter, we described how our focus on Knowledge Cartography led us to HCI research into participatory design, and particularly the role of facilitative practitioners in helping participants engage with creating representations of their designs and concerns. We talked about the choices that practitioners much make in the course of this work, arguing that it inherently involves aesthetic and ethical choices. We saw that although some PD literature addresses issues and concerns about representational practice and practitioner choice-making, there is a broad opportunity to go further in this area.

In the next chapter, we move deeper into the characteristics of those choices, outlining **a language to describe the distinctive experience and skillset** of participatory representational practitioners. Following that, we present five case study examples and discuss each in terms of these experiential dimensions. Lastly, we'll return to the themes with which we began, and discuss the implications for participatory design and education.

CHAPTER 3

Dimensions of Knowledge Art

In *Reflection in Action* (1983), Donald Schön articulated a challenge to researchers looking for ways to pull understanding of the professions away from rationalist concepts of expert practice. He critiqued the idea that "professionalism" consists of the ability to choose and apply techniques learned in school to prescribed types of situations. Schön insisted that there is artistry in professional practice, which although difficult to describe, nonetheless informs and shapes what practitioners actually do (1983: 49):

> Let us search … for an epistemology of practice implicit in the artistic, intuitive processes, which some practitioners do bring to situations of uncertainty, instability, uniqueness, and value conflict.

As the previous chapter described, to improve the facilitative aspect of PD practice, we need a fuller understanding of what participatory practitioners actually encounter—what they experience in the course of their practice. In this chapter we look at what an epistemology of participatory practice might consist of. We will start by taking a critical look at the idea of "practice" in general, focusing on the need to better understand its experiential dimensions. We will then look at each of these dimensions in some depth, relating them to the specific work of a facilitative practitioner working to engage participants with collaborative representations.

3.1   CRITICAL VIEWPOINTS ON PRACTICE RESEARCH

Much of the literature on professional practice is deficient in its understanding of practice in experiential terms. The literature around professional practice or "expert servicing" (Goffman, 1967, quoted in Aakhus, 2001) has a long tradition of critique of the idea that such practice can be understood, and progress made in the field, solely on the basis of techno-rational accounts (Schön, 1983). By this we mean that functionalist accounts offer prescriptive advice: actions of type A in situations of type B will result in outcomes of type C. These types of accounts are deficient in several ways:

- **They fail to describe experiential dimensions.** Prescriptive, techno-rational, or functionalist literature misses the texture of actual practitioner experience. By focusing on generalized or measurable phenomena, it obscures or avoids the subjectivity, messiness, and situation-specific nature of professional action. Especially missed is what constitutes the domain of aesthetic experience—the choices practitioners make in the shaping of their artifacts and discourses, in the ways they improvise and creatively respond to uncertainties and gaps in the smooth unfolding of their intended actions (Schön, 1983, 1987; Suchman, 2003).

- **They stay at the level of describing tools, methods, approaches, and outcomes.** Much research, in this view, stays at the instrumental or functionalist level, making the implicit argument that detailed analysis of tools and methods alone is enough to bring about desired outcomes, especially those assured by a tool or method's designer or advocate. Pick a technique or method, throw it at your participants and it will "perform" itself—the practitioner is just a neutral, albeit helpful, intermediary whose main function is to be almost invisible. But that is not the reality of most participatory situations in which the shaping and crafting role of someone guiding the process, or at least who's charged with making sure there is a positive outcome, is central to the events and results.

- **They do not address the aesthetics and ethics of practitioner choices at the moment-to-moment level.** Much research is neither contextual nor granular enough to adequately characterize the ways professional action always takes place in unique situations. Doing so requires looking at what actually happens in particular situations rather than only abstracting to general ones, and looking at specific events in the "heat" of actual practice—of moment-to-moment interactions and setbacks—in order to reveal what practitioners encounter and overcome.

We argue that approaches in the above traditions are not able to illuminate the "artistic, intuitive processes which some practitioners do bring to situations of uncertainty, instability, uniqueness, and value conflict"—processes that center around aesthetics, ethics, narrative, improvisation and sensemaking. Techno-rational approaches, or even tools-and-methods-centric accounts, are inadequate to the challenge laid down by Schön to develop an "epistemology of practice."[4]

A techno-rational approach would treat the work of a participatory representational practitioner as simply one of following established protocols, or unnecessary where it is assumed that meetings and participants can take care of themselves. Yet even when there are no so-called facilitators in a meeting, usually someone, however informally, takes on aspects of the role of ensuring that the meeting reaches its goals. If a knowledge construction task is to be done (as opposed to simply listening to someone else give a presentation), someone will often jump up and take notes on a flipchart or draw a diagram on a whiteboard. As used here, the term *practitioner* includes such informal leaders as well as paid professionals who come in to run the process and generate the products of a meeting.

---

[4] Chapter 3 in Selvin (2011) goes into more detail on this topic.

3.2   THE EXPERIENCE OF PARTICIPATORY PRACTICE

A number of theoretical strands help us explore these experiential dimensions of participatory practice. A recent stream of research uses concepts of "experience" to reframe the nature of design and tool use. For example, McCarthy and Wright (2004) propose that an individual's "felt experience," as well as Dewey's (1934) ideas of aesthetics, narrative, and subjectivity, provide a richer and more generative account of design moves and choices than available from cognitivist or social constructionist approaches. Bruner's (1990) narrative theory emphasizes the role of "breaches in the canonicity" of expected events, and the meanings of various kinds of repair attempted by an event's protagonists. Schön's (1983, 1987) work in understanding reflective practice in professional situations, particularly his emphasis on the artistry of practice, ties the aesthetic dimension into professional practices. Many research literatures, including mediation (e.g., Bush and Folger, 1994), group facilitation (e.g., Kolb et al., 2008), and group support systems (e.g., Bostrom et al., 1993), address ethical aspects of the practices and technologies involved in working with groups. Researchers connecting aesthetics with facilitative interventions, such as Cohen (1997), Salverson (2001), Alexander (2010), and Hilberry (2012) describe how the aesthetic dimensions of their practices (e.g., participatory creation of artistic artifacts and theater performances) serve, and in some cases undercut, the practices' transformative goals.

There is a need for theory and methods that can guide practitioner self-reflection by making actions and choices visible and amenable for discussion, analysis, and reflection (Zeiliger et al. 2008; Schön, 1983, 1987; Wagner and Piccoli, 2007). Practitioner competence is best understood at a granular level, examining situated facilitative competencies and their constituent elements (Stewart, 2006). Udsen and Jørgensen (2005) recommend exploring the particular and unique constellations of a person (e.g., a participatory practitioner), a particular set of "design materials" (e.g., the tools, methods, and representational artifacts a participatory practitioner works with), in specific "use contexts" (e.g., participatory representation-making sessions), taking care to "locate" practitioner actions and subjectivities rather than present them as a reified "master" discourse devoid of particularity (Suchman, 2003; Bardzell, 2010), or as elements of an abstracted "checklist" of desired behaviors (Wright et al., 2008; Boehner et al., 2008).

In the following section, we describe a model that allows us to examine instances of participatory representational practice carried out by practitioners of different skill levels and in different contexts, looking at the moves practitioners make in response to anomalies, the ways they strive to keep representations coherent, engaging, and useful, and how their shaping of representations connects to the way they are trying to be of service to their participants and to the larger effort.

3.3   AN EXPERIENTIAL MODEL

Using experience as a lens on practice brings to the foreground the "answerable engagement" a practitioner has with the other people in the situation of practice, which has both aesthetic and ethical dimensions. Such an orientation moves the focus of inquiry from objective and instrumental considerations to relational and creative ones. Following this argument, understanding the experience of participatory representational practice requires taking into account a complex constellation of people, tools, representations, surroundings, and other factors. These are summarized in the model shown in Figure 3.1.

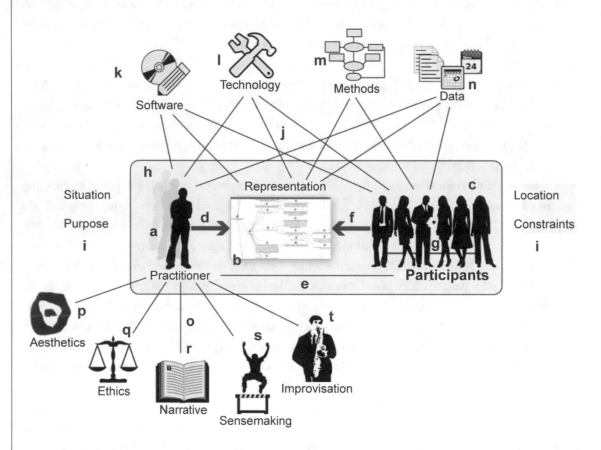

Figure 3.1: A model for understanding participatory representational practice.

The primary elements of the model are the people involved in creating the working materials and output of a participatory project, as seen at the center of the diagram. We've summarized the materials and outputs with the term "representation", and used as an example the kind of collaborative map described in Chapter 1 and used in many of the case studies in the following chapter.

In the model, the practitioner [a], who can be more than one person, orchestrates the participatory event and holds him or herself responsible for its success. He or she is concerned with the quality and clarity of representations [b] and the participants' [c] relationship to them. The practitioner takes primary responsibility for the form and content of a project's representations and the success of each participatory session or meeting within its context [i]. Varying levels of intervention can occur. The practitioners are not necessarily the ones with their hands on the equipment used to create representations; the model also addresses approaches where participants themselves do the representational work directly, though our primary focus in this book is on practices where a practitioner acts as an intermediary. The practitioner interacts with the representation [b] as well as with the participants [c]. The nature of this interaction varies with the context and the specific role(s) that practitioners play in the activity system of a session.

The representation [b] can be any sort of visual, textual, aural, or tactile type of representation. A few examples are free-form pictures, sticky notes, physical models, formal argument diagrams drawn on an easel sheet, and software-based idea maps. There can be multiple types of representation used in a session, including hand-written notes and action items. The participants [c] are the people in the room (whether a real or virtual space) taking part in the session. Being aware of and appropriately dealing with the diversity of participant personalities, relationships, and interests is a key practitioner skill, as well as an ethical imperative. Line [d] symbolizes the interaction of practitioners with the representation, which consists of actions on it (such as creating or modifying it), considering it, planning what to do with it, or even ignoring it. As with that of practitioners, participant interaction with the representation is best understood in a situated manner.

Line [e] shows the interaction of practitioner with participants. This can take many forms, even in a single session, such as facilitative interventions (keeping matters on track, making sure everyone is heard), questions and discussion, and process checks. It works both ways, as participants also interact with the practitioners in various ways. Line [f] is the interaction of the participants with the representation, which ranges from passive to active, from directly engaged with considering it and making changes to it to ignoring it or giving it occasional once-overs. Line [g] shows the interactions of participants with each other, from collegial to disputatious to side conversations.

The three primary elements (practitioner, representation, participants) are contained within box [h], symbolizing the boundaries of the session itself, such as a specific meeting. Some efforts may consist of a single session, where others comprise many sessions (which may include individual representational activities as well as collaborative ones). The session is in turn located within its surrounding context [i]. The context includes the overall project in which the representational activity is taking place, the specific locations where sessions are held (including whether they are face to face, virtual, or a combination); the situation that contains the session, such as the project of which the session is a part, the organizations involved, and the problem domain; the purpose of the session, and the constraints operating in the situation, such as time, budget, attention, or other resource limitations.

The lines [j] show the relations between the primary elements and what can be called the set of enablers: software [k], technology [l], methods [m], and data [n]. Each enabler is connected to each primary element, because all interact with each. Note that methods are not connected directly with the representation; methods are always filtered through a person's actions. Practitioners can use software [k] to operate on the representation; there can be multiple software packages in use (or none). Participants may also use the software. The software in turn runs on whatever technology platform [l] is in use, such as laptop or tablet computers. Technology also includes whatever display tools are being used, such as LCD projectors, virtual meeting or telepresence rooms, and voting keypads. Non-computer technology such as flip charts, newsprint sheets, markers, and whiteboards also count. During sessions, specific methods [m] will be employed, whether formal methods such as IBIS argument mapping or data flow diagrams, or informal methods like brainstorming or round-robin discussion. All of these operate on and draw from the data [n], that is the subject matter for the session, the conversations and ideas put forth and captured during the session, and any supporting material, such as reference information.

Finally, we arrive at the dimensions that inform an understanding of practice and the practitioner experience itself. Lines [o] show the aesthetics [p], ethics [q], narrative [r], sensemaking [s], and improvisation [t] associated with the work of the practitioner. Practitioner creativity can be seen in the ways they draw from these dimensions to foster, sustain, or restore participant engagement. These are described further in the following section.

3.4   EXAMINING THE DIMENSIONS

When people act as participatory practitioners, they inherently give form to their visual and other representational products [p]; make choices about how to proceed [q]; help establish meanings, motives, and causality [r]; and respond when something breaks the expected flow of events [s], often having to invent fresh and creative responses on the spot [t]. Choosing these dimensions as a focus for inquiry has both theoretical and methodological implications. Although they are presented as separate entities here for the purpose of description and analysis, in fact the dimensions commingle in the experience of practice.

The following sections describe each of these dimensions. As aesthetics is most absent from common discourse about group discussion and participatory practice, we cover it first.

3.4.1   AESTHETICS [p]   [5]

All participatory approaches have rules, whether explicit or implicit, about what constitutes a clear and expressive representation. People conversant with the approaches can quickly tell whether a particular representational artifact is a "good" example. This is the province of aesthetics. By including aesthetics in an analysis of practice, one may uncover aspects of practice that would be missed using more conventional or techno-rational approaches.

Aesthetics has to do with what human beings, in the moments when they are imparting expressive form via some medium (Arnheim, 1967), are actually doing: pulling together aspects of experience into a new whole that itself provides a shaped experience (Dewey, 1934). The aesthetic dimension of participatory practice is concerned with the shaping and crafting of representations in response to both immediate and context-specific imperatives (things that must be done to help achieve participant and project goals), as well as to implicit and explicit concepts of right form. Using the lens of aesthetics offers a unique perspective on the relationship of a practitioner to the participants, emphasizing process, collective and participatory expressive forms, even ethical and political concerns (Cohen, 1997). Understanding the aesthetic dimension of a participatory practitioner's work emphasizes how the encounter between participants, representations, and practitioner unfolds, the extent to which representation-building engages participants, and the ways in which participants are affected by the proceedings.

In explicitly incorporating the idea of aesthetics, we follow Dewey's (1934) argument that aesthetics is not an elite, esoteric, or rarefied concept, even though it is treated that way in common usage. Rather, aesthetic experience is to be understood as the high end of a continuum from prosaic experience; it is a paradigm for "true," unalloyed experience. Aesthetics govern how people would experience any situation if the diluting, dulling, oppressive, or conflictual aspects were stripped away (Dewey, 1934; McCarthy and Wright, 2004).

A commonplace conception of aesthetics has the term refer to ideas of beauty, particularly with regard to fine art, or to the ways screens look in an app or web page (Hartmann et al, 2008). But it has a broader meaning in psychology, philosophy, and evolutionary theory. These conceptions explore the aesthetic aspects of more everyday actions and artifacts. Studies in evolutionary biobehavior have shown that art and art-making have been a prominent feature in every period of human history, stretching back not only for the 2,000–3,000 years commonly thought of as the era of civilization, but in human settlements from more than 100,000 years ago (Dissanayake, 1988). Looking at art-making in this way positions aesthetics as a core human activity and concern, on a par with others such as religion and work, rather than the exclusive domain of highly trained artists operating in an "art world"—a central argument for Dewey (1934) as well.

---

[5] The image of an eye is taken from a Jean Arp woodcut, found on the cover of Arnheim (1967).

In these conceptions, art is no less about skill, but skill is in service to direct encounter with something of immediate importance and significance to the artist/practitioner and their community. It is skill that relies largely on intuition and a "feeling for phenomena and for action" (Schön, 1983: 241). As applied to professional practice of the type that occurs in the context of providing "expert servicing" (Aakhus, 2001) to a project and its stakeholders, an experiential approach goes against conventional understanding of expert skill as an application of prescribed behaviors in set ways. This is a subject of central concern to Schön's account of professional practice.

> Surely they [professionals and educators] are not unaware of the artful ways in which some practitioners deal competently with the indeterminacies and value conflicts of practice. It seems, rather, that they are disturbed because they have no satisfactory way of describing or accounting for the artful competence which practitioners sometimes reveal in what they do. (1983: 19)

Aesthetics are an inherent aspect of the work of any participatory practitioner that creates or engages participants in representations. They are especially evident in the seemingly intuitive and creative ways in which a participatory representational practitioner can respond to sudden or problematic situations. Attention to aesthetic aspects may reveal dimensions of practice that more techno-rational or behavioral lenses may miss. Practitioner aesthetics also has a direct relationship to ethical concerns, as we'll cover in the next section.

3.4.2   ETHICS [q]

> Professional ethics is concerned with the values appropriate to certain kinds of occupational activity…, which have been defined traditionally in terms of a body of knowledge and an ideal of service to the community; and in which individual professionals have a high degree of autonomy in their practice. (Chadwick, 1998)

The ethical dimension of participatory practice is concerned with the responsibilities of the practitioner to the other people involved in their situation of practice and with those people's various individual and collective needs, interests, goals, and sensibilities. In some situations, these responsibilities can be weighty in nature—for example, in situations of conflict or dispute, where every action and statement on the part of participants or practitioner holds the possibility of worsening the situation. In less fraught settings, consequences of action or inaction may be less severe, but can still have effects on the concerns of the participants or other stakeholders. Of particular concern for us are practitioner actions that affect the engagement of participants with each other, with the subject matter of their work, and with the nature and shaping of collaborative representations. These often can take the form of questions: Should I do action x or action y? What effect will it have on these participants if I do x? Should I intervene in their conversational flow? Or, Should I expend the effort to capture everything that person A is saying at this moment, or is the time better spent in cleaning up the map or preparing for the next activity?

Decisions about such actions often need to happen with extreme rapidity in a participatory practice context. In the heat of the moment, there is not time to hunker down and weigh the possible ethical effects of actions one might take. This does not lessen the fact that such choices are indeed ethical ones. The choices made reflect an a priori set of ethical concerns, and they have ethical consequences.

Of special concern here are treatments of how aesthetics meets ethics in professional practice, such as the need for aesthetic practitioners to be reflective about their practice (Salverson, 2001; Ellis, 2003; Hansen et al., 2007); and the need to balance a practitioner's aesthetic or personal goals with those of participants, clients, communities, audiences, co-workers, and other stakeholders (Alexander, 2010; DiSalvo et al., 2009; Sawyer, 1996, 2001; Dowmunt, 2003; Hansen et al., 2007; Small, 2009; Osthoff, 1997), as opposed to treating aesthetic choices as something an individual artist makes to satisfy their own tastes.

Simplistic conceptions of practitioner ethics (i.e., those that place emphasis on the techniques and tools rather than the active choice-making of practitioners) obscure the nature of practice in these situations and possibly limit the effectiveness of practitioners who subscribe to them. As ethnographic observations of other sorts of expert professional practice have shown (Levina, 2001; Dreir, 1993), characterizing the intersection of practitioners and clients as a group of disinterested actors pursuing a single unitary goal is an oversimplification. Rather, actors in problematic organizational situations always approach it and each other with a set of partially overlapping interests, goals, relationships, and concerns. Aakhus (2001: 362) argues that "neutrality" is not an adequate ethical self-conception for practitioners like dispute mediators to hold: "The rationale dispute mediators commonly use to explain their neutrality frustrates practitioners, stifles innovation for individuals and the profession, and obscures political dimensions of practice."

In Chapter 4, we will look at the ethical dimensions of practitioner choices given the situated web of relationships in each case study, examining at how the general stance of responsibility to participants and stakeholders plays out on the move-by-move level (Suchman, 2003). We attempt to discern or characterize the "values in action" and locate the practitioner actions within a normative framework (Friedman, 1996; Miller et al., 2007; Aakhus, 2007; Schön, 1983). We look for manifestations of practitioner empathy for participants, a key dimension of such ethics (Wright et al., 2008), and pay special attention to the ways the practitioners are responsive to others (Wright and McCarthy, 2008). We examine practitioner communication (both verbal and via the representations) in the way it does or does not aid mutual understanding, appreciation of the situation, and empathy (van Vuuren and Elving, 2008).

3.4.3 NARRATIVE [r]

The narrative dimension of practitioner experience concerns the connecting of diverse moments, ideas, and statements over time, as well as the human sense of causality and consequences—the narratives that we live within. Practitioner actions that have a narrative dimension—that serve to connect elements of the story being built in the representations for later telling and reading by others—contribute to the narrative shaping of both the effort itself and the representations that are the primary focus of their actions. These are the narratives we *construct*. Narrative is both a basic human developmental mechanism independent of any particular embodiment (Murray, 1995) and an aesthetic form that can be represented in oral, written, performed, or other forms. Narrative functions as a key human strategy for exploring and overcoming unexpected turns of events. Stories and story-making form a key psychological strategy for connecting disparate occurrences. This is particularly so when there is a break or disruption from an expected happening: "The function of the story is to find an intentional state that mitigates or at least makes comprehensible a deviation from a canonical cultural pattern" (Bruner, 1990: 49). Narrative frames human actions and lends explanation to the paradoxes and breaches that one encounters moving through life. In Wright and McCarthy's words, "narrative is a way of knowing that tolerates the existence of paradoxes in the text" (2008: 124).

The skill of the storyteller lies in the artfulness and effectiveness with which he or she can craft an artifact that makes sense of the "breaches in the ordinariness of life" (Bruner, 1990: 95). Narrative is a central means by which people are able to glue together bits of experience to construct a new understanding. It is also a key part of human development, a way that we learn to construct and communicate understanding of events and environments. Narrative is a central mechanism to confront surprise and the confounding of expectations. "The perpetual construction and reconstruction of the past provide precisely the forms of canonicity that permit us to recognize when a breach has occurred and how it might be interpreted" (Bruner, 1990).

Further, narrative is an intentional form—things that are created, with varying degrees of skill, to serve various purposes. We tell stories to explain the breaches in the ordinariness of life and put them into understandable contexts. Stories do not inhere in "reality." They are always creative constructions, sequences of events woven into what appears to be whole cloth, in the service of explicating some exception to the mundane. Descriptions of the mundane in and of themselves are not stories, unless they rise to include some breach and its consequences.

Bruner termed the ability to create meaning from events an "astonishing narrative gift" (1990: 96) that people use every day without intending or realizing it. Narrative enables coherence to be drawn and communicated in even the smallest interactions, even (perhaps especially) in one's communication with oneself, making sense of the events of a day and drawing them into some sort of acceptable ("mitigating," in Bruner's term) comprehensibility.

McCarthy and Wright (2004) point out that, as individuals, our interactions with technology can be understood through the prism of roles like author, character, protagonist, and co-producer. People are always actively engaging with technology as individuals who have their own aims, history, emotions, and creativity, as much as they are also embedded in a socio-historical context or attempting to perform some kind of task or composite activity.

While acknowledging that narrative provides an enveloping sociocultural frame for a participatory practitioner's work, our interests here focus on the more active and intentional stances and techniques that practitioners can take in service of the instrumental goals they and their participants have. Narrative is employed as an intentional strategy in a variety of professional practices. Among these are techniques such as narrative therapy, in which practitioners help their clients construct new life stories in order to come to fresh understanding of their agency, experiences, and possible new actions (Bruner, 1990; Murray, 1995; Payne, 2006). Narrative is used as a mediation strategy in dispute and conflict resolution settings (Lovelace, 2001). Understanding the ways narrative is used in these contexts helps shed light on the ways participatory practitioners weave various narrative strands and use intentional narrative techniques in their work, as well as providing a frame for understanding the practitioners' efforts to maintain the coherence and integrity of representations even in the face of interruptions and potential derailments of their sessions (Yoong and Gallupe, 2002). Narrative also lies at the core of the kinds of hypermedia representations we describe in the following chapter, providing associations between disparate elements in the service of various themes and adding the dimension of temporality. Narrative itself can be thought of as hypertextual—a gluing together of moments in time accomplished in a visual medium, stressing associations and relationships. The narrative quality of a hypermedia practitioner's moves is manifested in their manipulations of nodes, links, and transclusions, providing explanations and supplementing earlier points, as well as creating structures that will be of use for future "readings" and "writings".

Narrative analysis provides a frame for understanding practitioner efforts to maintain the coherence of representations even in the face of interruptions and potential derailments within sessions. For example, what is the intended arc of events? How is that arc meaningful to the participants? What roles do the various parties play and how are those important within the surrounding situation? As well as looking at this encompassing framing, we will also look at the ways breaches of the expected occur, and how the practitioner as protagonist reacts to these. We will examine the narrative aspects of the participatory representations, and how changes to them relate to the other narrative levels at play in and around a session.

Some might call what we are calling "narrative" here as simply "context"—but it's more than that. Narrative is what gives context its shape and direction. People, both individually and collectively, are always tending towards something. Events follow events, and actions shape events, in the service of moving events towards some kind of goal, shape, or direction. Narrative is what describes that larger movement—what might be called the movement that shapes the moves, or the context for the context.

3.4.4   SENSEMAKING [s]

The previous section described how narrative theory emphasizes the human experience of encountering breaches in expectation and causality. Narrative understanding is an important source for sensemaking processes (Johansson and Heide, 2008). Sensemaking theory examines what happens at the moment of encounter with a breach. Researchers from a variety of fields are increasingly attempting to understand what occurs when people encounter situations characterized by instability, unpredictability, overload, and other factors that prevent, even temporarily, smooth and predictable progressions of stimulus and action.

Several definitions of sensemaking appear in the literature. Some researchers treat sensemaking as largely in the province of information retrieval: there is a problem or question, a body of information that relates to it that one has acquired (or has been thrust into) through some means, and there is a need to develop an understanding of it (e.g., Russell et al., 1993; Klein et al., 2006). Such research, which largely focuses on tools and people as users of those tools, has a tendency to treat the human dimensions of sensemaking in a somewhat uniform, or even mechanistic manner. Given certain types of situations and certain types of tools, people are seen to respond and behave in certain ways that can be more or less aided by different sorts of a priori approaches. Another, only partially related, vein of sensemaking research is more generally a qualitative or phenomenological approach. This has more to do with the human experience of being brought up against a discontinuity of some kind, something that prevents a person from moving forward as they want or need to do. This conception is identified in large part with Brenda Dervin (1983, 1992, 1997, 1998; Dervin and Naumer, 2009) but also related to the broader organizational sensemaking described by Karl Weick (1995; Weick et al., 2005; Weick and Meader, 1993), in which the ways in which people in groups and organizations encounter disasters and catastrophes play a large role.

Dervin's model posits that sensemaking occurs when an obstacle (a "gap" in Dervin's terminology) stops or frustrates a person in their progress through "time-space" and stymies their efforts to continue. In order to resume progress, the person needs to design a movement (a bridge) around, through, over, or away from the obstacle. This can be as simple as asking someone for directions or help, or as complicated as a set of actions that may have a trial-and-error character.

> As an individual moves through an experience, each moment is potentially a sense-making[6] moment. The essence of that sense-making moment is assumed to be addressed by focusing on how the

---

[6] Dervin uses the term "sense-making" rather than the more common "sensemaking." From personal correspondence (2011): Dervin "purposively uses the hyphen to mark sense-makings as verbings. Dervin's "Sense-Making" is a methodology for studying internal and external behaviors she labels as sense-making, sense-unmaking. She includes in sense-makings and sense-unmakings (phenomena) all the verbings humans do in internal; and external communicatings, individually and collectively. Information processing and all its variations; as well as knowledge-making and all its variations are among these."

actor defined and dealt with the situation, the gap, the bridge, and the continuation of the journey after crossing the bridge. (Dervin, 1992: 69-70)

These sensemaking actions can be understood as attempting to answer a set of tacit questions: What is stopping me? What can I do about it? Where can I look for assistance in choosing and taking an action? Weick and Meader (1993: 232) define sensemaking as the process of constructing "moderately consensual definitions that cohere long enough for people to be able to infer some idea of what they have, what they want, why they can't get it, and why it may not be worth getting in the first place."

Although in some ways sensemaking can be thought of as a perpetual, ongoing process (Weick, 1995), it is also something placed in sharp relief by encountering surprise, interruption, or "whenever an expectation is disconfirmed" (Weick, 1995: 14). Schön characterizes such moments in professional practice as situations of "complexity, instability, and uncertainty," laden with "indeterminacies and value conflicts" (1987: 19). Such moments are further defined by a "density of decision points" (Sawyer, 2003: 145). In professional practice, the moments where sensemaking comes to the fore can have the character of impasses (Aakhus, 2003) or dilemmatic situations (Tracy, 1989; see also Aakhus, 2001).

Sensemaking moments are not of any inherent length. Schön refers to the time-scale of such moments as the "action-present":

... the zone of time in which action can still make a difference to the situation. The action-present may stretch over minutes, hours, days, or even weeks or months, depending on the pace of activity and the situational boundaries that are characteristic of the practice. (1983: 62)

Schön's conception of reflection-in-action "hinges on the experience of surprise." An expert professional is able to respond to this with an artful, sophisticated exploration of the "understanding which he surfaces, criticizes, restructures and embodies in further action." (1983: 50) The professional engages in a "conversation with the situation." Aakhus characterizes this as a "design" activity (2003). There is also an aesthetic dimension, which Cohen finds in Peirce's epistemological concept of "abduction": "Abduction functions in 'ordinary' perception, as when the mind struggles to get a grasp on a scene, and finally, as in a flash, the connection and harmony become apparent" (Cohen, 1997: 186).

Representation-making, whether physical or mental, is central to sensemaking responses. Russell et al. (1993) point out that "representation design is central to the sensemaking enterprise" and, when engagement occurs in a "learning loop" of refining representations, this can "reduce the cost of task operations, changing the sensemaking cost and gain structures." Creating representations is in itself often a way to help negotiate and construct a shared understanding (Weick and Meader, 1993) of a situation or project as a whole. Within this larger frame, the act of representation itself engenders both negotiation and confusion, when the tools and discourse lose, if even momentarily, a clear sense of fit. This requires consideration of how people determine meaning and orientation in the face of uncertainty, especially when there are multiple or competing perspectives on what is going on, coupled with pressure and constraints on resources that might help make sense of an equivocal situation (Muhren et al., 2008). Applications of sensemaking research include work on creating better tools and representations to aid individual sensemakers in the context of information retrieval (Russell et al. 1993), naturalistic decision-making (Klein et al., 2006), organizational communication (Weick, 1995; Johansson and Heide, 2008), audience and user studies (Dervin and Naumer, 2009), the role of artifacts in organizational knowledge (Shariq, 1998), and management (Kurtz and Snowden, 2003).

In Chapter 4, we will look at the particular character of participatory practitioner sensemaking, especially as it is expressed through moves on representations, explorations of and changes to them, and interactions with participants about them (Selvin and Buckingham Shum, 2008, 2009). We consider in what ways representations, and the practitioners' interactions with them, contain both a source of obstacles and impasses, and a means of resolving or addressing them.

The actions of a skilled practitioner at sensemaking moments differ from those of a novice or less skilled actor in the depth and quality of the reflection-in-action, aesthetic engagement, and rapidity of effective response that occur. The moments can extend in physical time. Focusing on the sensemaking actions of a participatory representational practitioner may illuminate both the nature of skilled practice in this medium and lay out directions and options for future research and professional development.

In the following section, we look at what skilled practitioners do at sensemaking moments. When their tools, methods, or pre-planned processes fail them (even temporarily)—they improvise.

3.4.5   IMPROVISATION [t]

While some aspects of participatory practice follow predetermined patterns and draw on techniques and methods planned in advance, skilled practitioners often find themselves switching to alternative sensemaking strategies, or even improvising. It is the degree of creativity and spontaneity employed at this point that distinguishes the *improvisational* dimension of action from other sorts of sensemaking activities. Improvisation can be discerned in the freshness and innovativeness of the response to an event that triggers sensemaking.

Improvisation is rarely a focus for research in the HCI, CSCW, hypermedia, and group support systems (GSS) fields. Even in fields like teaching or semiotics, despite their focus on the highly improvisational world of human speech, studies of improvisational aspects are relatively few and far between (Sawyer, 1996). Improvisation is difficult to control for or measure in laboratory or outcome-based studies of software tool use. Some research into meeting behavior, such as the use of GSS technologies, tends to regularize the practices surrounding the technology (Aakhus, 2001, 2004), analogous to similar moves to "script" teacher-student interactions (Sawyer, 2004) and otherwise de-skill or de-emphasize the creative aspects of many sorts of professional practices (Schön, 1983). Yet improvisation is not just a metaphor for what occurs in the encounter of participants, practitioners, context and tool use; rather, improvisation is core to a grounded theory of situated social action for such encounters (Sawyer, 1997).

Sawyer (1999) discerns three levels at which to understand improvisation: individual (improvisation on the part of particular actors), group (improvised interactions within a bounded, particular situation), and cultural ("the pre-existing structures available to performers—these often emerge over historical time, from broader cultural processes;" 1999: 202). The cultural level supplies the elements of a practitioner's *repertoire* (Schön, 1983), the collection of preexisting techniques and concepts (whether learned in school or from work or other experiences), which Schön terms the "scope of choice" containing what the practitioner draws from, combines, and invokes in the heat of an encounter. Practitioners of exceptional skill often possess repertoires of great range and variety (Schön, 1983), which they are capable of combining in innovative, expressive, and subtle ways.

Maintaining an awareness of the emergent aspects of a situation, however, does not mean that all is left to chance. Sawyer (2004: 12) emphasizes the concept of "disciplined improvisation," which juxtaposes improvisational aspects of practice (dialogue, sensemaking responses, spontaneous and creative acts) with "overall task and participation structures," such as "scripts, scaffolds, and activity formats." Skilled practitioners are able to navigate judiciously between moments when they can rely on pre-existing structure and scripted actions, and moments calling for fresh responses and combinations. In a participatory design session, improvisation can take many forms, such as sudden shifts in stance or tool strategy. Often, these are mini-improvisations that occur and conclude rapidly, unplanned, and not referred to verbally in the course of other sorts of actions. We will see several examples of these in the following chapter's case studies.

Degrees or levels of improvisational mastery can be observed in different practitioners. Furnham (2003) cites Frost and Yarrow's (1990) use of the term *disponsibilite* as a capacity of availability, openness, readiness, and acceptance; "the condition improvisers aspire to … having at one's fingertips the capacity to do or say what's appropriate." This distinguishes what could be called "intentional" improvisation—that entered into intentionally as a part of a known practice—from the inherent improvisation that all people do as part of everyday actions like verbal conversation. Expert improvisers are able to marshal the bits of routines, motifs, structures, and frameworks they have learned (Sawyer, 2004) and assembled from experience and immersion in their medium. Beginners or apprentices will have neither this broad repertoire to choose from nor the experience to know what combinations might work in various situations (Sawyer, 1999). This only comes from having the ability to "devote the sustained attention to internalizing an improvisational tradition."

Schön (1983) illustrates this in his description of the mastery displayed by jazz drummers. They work in a constantly changing environment in which their fellow performers can take a piece of music off in an unexpected manner at any moment. They exhibit a "feel for the material," making "on the spot judgments" about how to read the schema at work and choose from their "repertoire of musical figures." The elements get "varied, combined, and recombined" to "give coherence to the performance." As the musicians around them make shifts in direction, each player "feels" the new direction, makes "new sense of it," and adjusts accordingly. To get to this point of expertise requires years of perfecting technique and building up a variety of elements to draw from, as well as the sensitivity to know which kinds of contributions will add to the whole, support the other players, and be fresh and authentic, not rote.

In the absence of a structured or pre-scripted template for managing (at times fraught) conversational interactions, facilitative practitioners must themselves improvise the scope, nature, and tempo (frequency and depth) of their interventions in the participants' discursive flux and flow. Beyond this regulatory role, they also need (if it is situationally appropriate) to "notice and comment on connections" (Sawyer, 2004: 15) between participants and with the content. This requires the ability to maintain "coherence with the current state of the interactional frame" (Sawyer, 1997) as well as looking for opportunities to contribute their own insights on items of relevance or points of connection in the discourse or surrounding context.

Studying the role of improvisation in skilled professional practice requires an emphasis on the character of practitioner actions in the face of difficult, unusual, or complex situations. Differentiating the expert from the novice, Schön argues, is the expert's ability to act effectively when being spontaneous without having to (or being able to) plan their actions in advance—acting with a rapidity and spontaneity that "confounds" the less skilled (Schön, 1983). The "artful competence" that expert practitioners can display inheres in just this ability to respond to a situation's complexity "in what seems like a simple, spontaneous way" (Schön, 1983), often drawing from elements only available in the immediate surroundings. For Nachmnanovitch (1990), this shows the expert improviser as a *bricoleur*, an "artist of limits," taking bits of the situation, combining them with their repertoire of readymades, and creating something of unique relevance to the needs of the situation.

A key property of improvisation in a situation is its emergent character—situations or moments where the outcome cannot be predicted in advance and the actors do not know the meanings of their actions until others respond (Sawyer, 2004; Aakhus, 2003: 284). For situations like participatory practice, this can be further characterized as collaborative emergence, in the sense that "no single participant can control what emerges; the outcome is collectively determined by all participants" (Sawyer, 2004). In the realms of facilitation and mediation, where there is a practitioner helping a group of people (whose interests may be divergent) work together towards some common purpose, holding an orientation towards the situation's emergent character is an important ethical stance (Bush and Folger, 1994). Practitioner intentions themselves should be emergent, based on the discovery of the actual (and often shifting) nature of the situation (Aakhus, 2003).

The experiential dimension of improvisation describes how practitioners deal with unexpected events in the course of a participatory representational session. Although improvisation is rarely a focus for research in the HCI, CSCW, hypermedia, and GSS fields, there is a broad literature that examines the role and nature of improvisation in a number of fields. Skilled improvisers draw on "repertoires" and "readymades," and have a broader scope of choice than those with less skill. Improvisation has its own ethical implications in various practices.

3.5   SUMMARY

This chapter has described the need for experiential understanding of participatory representational practice and presented a framework for that understanding, consisting of five main dimensions. It described each as areas of inquiry with special attention to their implications for studying professional practice.[7] Figure 3.2 summarizes the discussion.

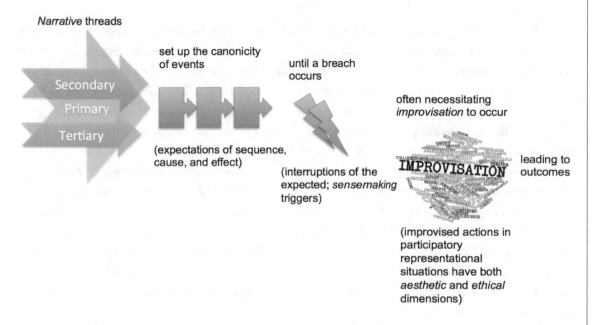

Figure 3.2: Summarizing the experiential dimensions of representational practice.

Once we understand how aesthetics, narrative, sensemaking, improvisation, and ethics underlie the choices representational practitioners make, the next question becomes how to see those dimensions at work for practitioners, participants, and the representations they create. We have found it helpful to understand each dimension as characterizing a form of *action*.

---

[7] See Selvin (2011: 74–112) for an extended discussion of how the dimensions are treated in the research literature on computing, practitioner studies, reflective practice, participatory design, facilitation, mediation, and art-making as an applied practice.

Aesthetics is acting to create meaningful representational forms. Creating any desired form, even building a network or working on a car engine, involves considerations of right form.[8] To see aesthetics in action, look for the form that representations take, how ideas are put into tangible visual, textual, and aural form. How do those forms reflect the needs, concerns, and abilities of the people involved? How do the forms depict the subjects they refer to? How expressive are they?

Narrative is acting to create a story, as well as acting within a story (a series of events) or acting out a story. To see narrative in action, you look for the way events and actions connect, the way a representational session moves from start to finish, the way events are understood within the session (which are expected and which appear as anomalous in some way), and what kinds of considerations guide the way events and actions unfold. What are the stories each participant brings to the proceedings? How do they connect or diverge? What are the assumptions or desires different actors hold about the way things should unfold?

Sensemaking is acting in the face of anomaly, uncertainty, or doubt. To see sensemaking in action, look for the "breaches in the canonicity" of events, moments where the expected course of a session did not run smoothly, where anomalies occurred that prevented or impeded smooth or expected functioning—whether briefly or for an extended period. Look for how people respond to, understand, and (if successful) move past the events or stimuli that triggered sensemaking. In what ways did sensemaking triggers disrupt the flow of events, take people off course, or confound expectations?

Improvisation is acting without a net, script, or recipe. To see improvisation in action, look for the spontaneous, unplanned actions people take, often in the face of sensemaking triggers. Look for the ways unplanned acts build on each other and how they address or resolve the events that launched them. Look for the reasons improvised actions were necessary or desirable in that context. Why couldn't or didn't the actor choose pre-planned actions, techniques, or methods? Why at these moments did they choose to act in an unplanned manner? What specific form did the improvised actions take, drawing on what skills, insights, or relationships to the people and particularities of the situation?

Ethics are actions that affect others. To see ethics in action, look for the kinds of choices people make in the way they speak and act in terms of the effect on other people[9] (whether those people are present in the immediate situation or not). What informs those choices, whether abstract principles or specific (even impulsive) interactions in the moment? What do actors choose to foreground, emphasize, and pay attention to, or conversely keep in the background or ignore? How do these choices affect others involved in the situation, whether immediately in the moment or at some later point in time?

---

[8] "The intelligent mechanic engaged in his job, interested in doing well and finding satisfaction in his handiwork, caring for his materials and tools with genuine affection, is artistically engaged." (Dewey, 1934: 4)

[9] Although in this discussion we are primarily referring to actions that affect other people, there can be equally important ethical implications of one's actions towards the environment, animals, institutions, oneself, etc.

The following chapter shows how to locate and understand these dimensions when looking at instances of participatory representational practice.

CHAPTER 4

Case Studies

What do sports coaches look for when they watch films of games? They search out the ways in which players respond to changes and obstacles, the small moves that end up making the difference in a game, so that they can point out to their players how to spot opportunities. They look not only for "direct" observables like talent, athleticism, and skills, but also more intangible factors like character, interactional styles, and the way teammates encourage each other. Similarly, chess players study each move of famous games to discover how champions react to unexpected challenges, and how they employ style, technique, and attitude to adjust their play to the demands of a specific game.

Generally, the literature on participatory design and related sorts of facilitation does not contain such views of practitioner moves and choices, but we feel they are a source of insight in how to create and sustain engagement in participatory activities and representations. To make them meaningful and effective, representational activities must be composed of moves and choices made in response to the shifting landscape, to open up the possibility that innovation and creativity will happen.

Think of this chapter as some training videos for facilitating PD through representational engagement, with examples of practitioner moves that either facilitated or inhibited participant engagement, and a set of ways of characterizing them for analysis and discussion. The five "instant replays" contain illustrative incidents that reveal how the experiential dimensions were at work, with what consequences for the practitioners and participants involved. We look especially closely at the moves practitioners make that fostered, sustained, restored, or eroded participant engagement with collaborative representations. We'll use the concepts developed in the previous chapter to "read" actual instances of participatory practice in experiential terms.

This chapter contains case studies of actual representational sessions of various kinds, in which we look closely at sensemaking triggers that occurred in real sessions, and the actions that the practitioners took in response to those triggers. Some of the actions were successful (in terms of getting a session back on track, or keeping the momentum going despite what could have been a problem), and some weren't. The case studies were mostly derived from close analysis of video recordings of sessions.[10] In each, we look at the narrative framing of the session (what was going on, who were the participants and practitioners, what were the various goals, roles, and expectations), and examine what kinds of sensemaking triggers occurred. We then look at what the practitioners

---

[10] Several analysis methods are described in the Appendix.

did in terms of combinations of moves and choices, and analyze them from the perspectives of the experiential dimensions discussed in Chapter 3.

Five case studies are presented.

1. Tom and Jackie: A mother devising a representational game to help a young boy understand how a compass works.

2. Contingency Planning: Enabling a risk assessment exercise to be completed accurately under pressure.

3. Hab Crew: Completing a science mission planning knowledge map in the form needed by a remote collaborating team.

4. Ames Group 4: Engaging a group of workshop attendees to directly participate in creating an issue map, with close collaboration between two practitioners.

5. Ames Group 2: An attempt to restore focus on a collaborative representation in a workshop.

The five cases feature different sorts of contexts, sensemaking moments, and practitioner responses. We begin with one that is "close to home," and will be familiar to parents. It occurred spontaneously one afternoon in the kitchen of one of the authors while the other was visiting.

4.1   EXAMPLE 1: TOM AND JACKIE—AN IMPROVISED EDUCATIONAL GAME

In this first example, we see a mother, Jackie, improvising a game to help teach her young son Tom how to use a new compass he'd just been given. In the course of the episode, she develops rules and decides which kinds of representational moves her son can make. Jackie instantaneously devises a "plan" that combined an easy-to-understand activity, fun, but also learning. It involved showing Tom an engaging representation, inviting him to shape it according to the (instant) rules of the game, and giving him guidance along the way in terms of what actions he could or couldn't take within the context.[11]

Young Tom, six years old, had been given a small, round black compass by his parents. He was excited and ran off from the lunch table to experiment. Not long after he came back into the kitchen, on the verge of tears. "I don't understand what it means," he mourned. "The little needle moves all over the place. How does it help me find things?" His mother, Jackie, said, "It's not that hard, Tom. I'll show you." She took some brass badges out of a drawer, and put them on the kitchen table. Tom sat down in the chair next to her. "Now let's pretend this one is Sally's house," she said, pointing at one of the badges, "and this one is the school. Where would the park be?" He moved

---

[11] For a video capturing part of this episode, see http://vimeo.com/69912504.

one of the badges near the "school". "That's right!" she said. "Now put the compass in the middle of them where our house would be." Jackie took Tom's hand, the one clutching the little compass, and moved it to the table between the objects. He put it down. Jackie pointed at the "school" and said, "Which letter on the compass is closest to the school?" "E", Tom said. "That's right, E is east, so that means that the school is east of our house. What about the park?" "S", Tom said. "So which direction is the park from us?" "South," Tom said, beginning to smile.

Figure 4.1: Summary of the Tom and Jackie sensemaking episode.

She moved one of the badges to the lower left, and asked, "Now which direction is that?" "South… west," said Tom, smiling. "Southwest." "Southwest, that's right," his mum said. "What if it's… west east?" he said. "You can't get west east," she replied, pointing at the compass so he could see that the two directions were on opposite sides. He laughed. "Where's Luke's house?" asked his father. "He's on Peel Road," Tom answered. "Can you point? Where do you think Luke's house is, in relation to our house?" asked his father. "It would be…" Tom started. She handed him a pen lid, saying "here you go, show us where Luke's house is."

She pointed at one of the badges. "This is where our house is, show us where Luke's house is." "Mummy can I just have a piece of paper?" Tom asked. "No, do it with the pen lid," she said. "Where's Luke's house?" He smiled and first pushed the lid farther away on the table. "No, it's not over there", she said, while Tom laughed. "Which way do we walk to get to Luke's house?" He then put it more carefully to the left of the compass. "That's right, so which way are we going to get to Luke's house?" "North," Tom said, smiling confidently. She pointed at her plate from lunch, farther to the left on the table. "Now Mummy's plate is school, which way do we walk to school?" "North," he said. "There you go!" she declared.

4.1.1 DISCUSSION

The primary narrative thread in this episode concerns a happy weekend day, suddenly interrupted by Tom's frustration at not understanding how his compass worked. Jackie wanted to help Tom deal with the issue, learn something, and have fun doing it. She had an instant, unplanned inspiration—an improvisation—to use the little brass badges and make it into a game. She decided how the objects would play into the representation, making aesthetic choices with simple but clear tactile and visual rules, deciding on the fly on a compelling and engaging form that Tom could understand, enter into and be part of. She got him to point to and move the objects around, to engage in the representation and in its evolution. She improvised a "script" for the game that contained a rising set of demands on Tom's skills and evolving knowledge, crafting an inner narrative for the game with actions that had sequences and meanings. She made decisions—ethical choices—about what Tom should pay attention to, and what he could do and not do with the representation.

For example, a sensemaking trigger for Jackie came when Tom asks if he can just draw the way to Luke's house on paper, rather than continuing to use the badges. This was a challenge (however small) to the assumed flow of events characterizing the game to that point. Jackie could have acquiesced to Tom's sudden wish to use paper, but she chose to keep the same representational strategy they had been using. As we'll see with the other case studies, it's not that this was an inherently "right" or "wrong" choice, nor is it our interest here to assess rightness or wrongness. Rather, we seek to point out where such choices occur, analyze what experiential factors were at work, and describe what the consequences were within the specific, situated context of that episode.

Jackie was sweet to Tom throughout, but also kept him firmly "on task" long enough for Tom to grasp the principles of the compass and understand how it could tell him directions between things he cared about. In doing this, Jackie helped Tom make sense of something that had been frustrating him, turning it into something he could enjoy and take forward into life.

Of special interest is the immediacy of the responses Jackie makes to the events of the episode: the instant creation of the visual game, the way she devises rules on the fly and makes decisions about which ones to enforce in what way. What had been a happy event just a little earlier in the day—when Tom was given the compass—now presented itself as a problem that needed to be solved, when he came in to the kitchen upset that he didn't understand it. It was also an educational opportunity, the kind parents are alert to: to learn how to do something, bringing their child back to happiness when upset but to do so without coddling or spoiling, to expand Tom's horizons by learning something but without stultifying. The canonicity of the primary narrative—a happy Sunday afternoon at home with the family—was restored.

4.2   EXAMPLE 2: CONTINGENCY PLANNING—A PARTICIPANT TAKES OVER

Moving into more formal participatory knowledge representation activities, the second case examines a moment in a corporate contingency planning exercise when a participant decides to take over the proceedings.[12]

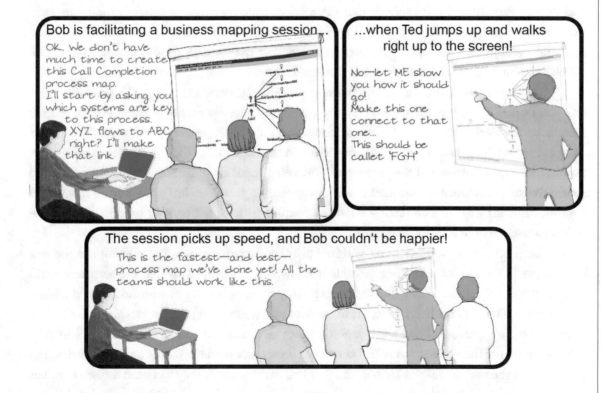

Figure 4.2: Summary of contingency planning sensemaking episode.

---

[12] For a longer treatment, see http://oro.open.ac.uk/28678/.

The context was a risk assessment exercise for a large telecommunications firm. A team faced a tight deadline to create models of its five core business processes (Ordering, Billing, Provisioning, Call Completion, and Emergency Communications), analyzing which groups, systems, and tasks were involved in each, so as to be able to develop contingency plans in case major systems failed. To compound the problem, all of the process models had to be constructed by different teams of participants working in parallel, one for each major process. It was up to the small team of practitioners to put a method in place to ensure consistency of approach. Many of the systems, tasks, and groups played different roles across the five processes, so it was of central importance to be able to show the connections across the processes. For example, if a system named ABC, used by group DEF, played a role called GHI in the Emergency Communications process, but played a role called JKL in the Billing process used by a group MNO, the collection of process maps would need to clearly reflect that.

The role of the practitioners was to convene the working teams, build up the process models using a hypertext idea-mapping tool by getting direct input and validation from the team members, and do this rapidly and accurately so that the models could be cross-validated in the three-week timeframe for the project as a whole. It was of particular importance that the practitioners followed a careful method to ensure that the objects representing the systems, people, and tasks could be queried to show all of the other processes that used them.

Because of the complexity of the business processes involved (as well as the pressure everyone was under), there was often disagreement among the participants about the way each process should be mapped, and even the ways to characterize the roles, systems, and tasks. There were disagreements about the level of granularity to use in the depictions. Many participants even questioning the exercise itself and the amount of time being spent on it. Readers who have performed facilitative roles in similar circumstances will recognize this phenomenon: many people, many constraints, different ways of interpreting a task, all coupled with an overarching need to perform the task effectively within a short timeframe.

The practitioners were working within a primary narrative of needing to complete the risk assessment in the face of a looming possible disruption to operations, so that the company could prioritize its contingency plans. But there were many other narratives at work. Each of the business processes themselves had thousands of workers and millions of customers who worked on or were affected by them, and had large ongoing teams operating on, monitoring, and dedicated to improving them. The various teams had their own organizational imperatives and trajectories. The practitioners themselves did not know each other before the project. They had been thrown together to develop and carry out the risk assessment methodology. Previous efforts had floundered in the face of the size of the effort and time and other pressures (not least of which were diverging ideas about how to carry it out).

These exigencies forced a unique constellation of ethical imperatives on the practitioner team. Although they needed the involvement, expertise, knowledge, and participation of the working teams, they had to keep the mapping process intact and effective. There would not be time to redo. Each mapping session had to be driven to closure within the allotted timeframe. This meant that the practitioners could not allow much time for exploratory moves ("Is this the best way to do the risk assessment?") or disagreement ("We shouldn't say ABC does GHI in MNO, it does PQR"). They needed to force consensus, to interrupt of the discussion started to veer off topic ("Hey, shouldn't we add some new features to ABC?"), and to forestall meta-discussion ("Why are we spending our time on this?" "What is the company trying to accomplish?"), even if they might otherwise preferred to have facilitated such discussions and explored the issues more broadly. Frequently, the practitioner team needed to recognize when the discussion began to move off the intended course, improvising interventions to get things back on track, all while maintaining a respectful and collegial tone to the proceedings. Keeping things within narrowly defined boundaries while still getting effective, involved participation from all the individuals—not an easy balance to strike!

One incident from these proceedings provides a good example of on-the-fly practitioner sensemaking, improvisation, and choice-making. While many of the sessions had required heroic efforts on the part of the practitioners to keep participants focused and engaged in the mapping work, in this case the opposite occurred. It happened at a mapping session for a process named Call Completion, which concerned which systems and tasks were involved when customers placed voice calls through the telephony network (an activity that happens millions of times each minute). This session took place in a basement room at the company headquarters, which served as a crisis communications center during natural disasters and the like.

The session had started like all the others. The practitioners introduced the mapping method and started querying the participants for steps, tasks, groups, and systems, constructing the mapping representation and asking for validation. They continually directed the participants to look at the screen and ensure that they were capturing and representing their input correctly. But then an unusual thing happened. One of the participants, Ted, who had been intently following the practitioners' representational actions, suddenly jumped up and walked directly to the large projection screen. He started pointing at the icons and objects on the screen, even touching them on the screen as if to grab and move them himself. He started directing the practitioners how to label, place, and link them together, how the lines should be drawn, and where the groups of nodes should be moved on the map. He inserted himself directly into the construction of the map to a far greater degree than normal—certainly greater than the often "pulling teeth" character of practitioner and participant interactions that had characterized some of the other sessions. Generally, participants in the project had left the work involved in the construction of the representation to the practitioners, except for making verbal contributions. But Ted felt that things were moving too slowly, and he wanted to be directly involved in the representational shaping.

When this happened, the practitioners faced a choice. Should they insist on maintaining their usual direct control of the representation, or should they cede control to Ted? In this case, the practitioners made the instant (improvised) decision to shift their role from "leading" the representational work, to being "in service" to this suddenly super-engaged participant. They still had their hands on the laptop housing the idea mapping software, but they now let Ted run the show. In doing so, they changed their facilitative emphasis to be keeping up with Ted's energetic directions, and inviting the other participants to validate what Ted was doing. This was an ethical choice—to shift their role and cede direct control—as well as an aesthetic one—allowing Ted's manipulations to change the way items were being arranged on the screen, rather than their own. These choices were improvised, in response to a sensemaking trigger—Ted's jumping up and taking control—within the overall set of narratives guiding and informing the session.

In this case, the outcome was an exceptionally compelling map. For the remainder of the session, the practitioners made small suggestions and course corrections to Ted's moves, to ensure consistency and coherence, but otherwise let him drive the proceedings. The episode also helped shape later sessions with other groups, because now the practitioners could hold out an effective example of participant engagement to the other working teams ("It works best when you get up and tell us what the map should look like!"). Thus, this episode altered the subsequent narrative framing of the later sessions.

4.2.1   DISCUSSION

As experienced facilitators are aware, it can often be a struggle to get participants to focus on a representational task, especially one involving an unfamiliar method, rather than just talking to (or arguing with) one another about the topic. Often, the representation, especially in the messy form it can often take in the process of creation (e.g., while being hand-written on an easel sheet or whiteboard before being cleaned up later), is less compelling—and slower to emerge—than just talking to one another would be. People are extremely good at ideating and verbally discussing with great rapidity—but often less good (and less patient) at creating a careful, deliberate, shared visual representation. Having a participant enthusiastically embrace the representational task—in this case—was a happy surprise, and the practitioner choice to allow and encourage it, an easy one to make.

The next example looks closely at a complex, condensed set of representational moves made in close collaboration between practitioner and participants. It goes into a greater level of move-by-move detail in the construction of a portion of a knowledge map as part of a large, ongoing project.

4.3   EXAMPLE 3: HAB CREW—COLLABORATIVE RETRIEVAL AND AUTHORING

In this case, a science team had to create a plan for a geological exploration within an hour-long session, as part of a months-long project involving many teams.[13] Unlike the previous two cases, both practitioner and participants were part of an intact project team used to working together. They had done similar exercises using the same tools and processes many times before. In this episode, they confront a gap in the knowledge representation they were working on, and engage in an unplanned rapid collaborative exploration of their issue map repository to find the solution.

Figure 4.3: Summary of Hab Crew sensemaking episode.

[13] For more details, see Clancey et al., 2005; Sierhuis and Buckingham Shum, 2008; and Selvin, 2011.

The episode took place as part of a NASA field trial of robotic rovers, held in the Utah desert at the Mars Desert Research Station, or MDRS. The specific session was one of several during a multi-week project, in which a crew of scientists at the MDRS created plans for the next day's work with the rovers. The plans were referred to as Extra-Vehicular Activities, or EVAs. The scientists were simulating a Mars mission, even to the extent of putting on space suits when they left the "Hab" (the habitat they lived in during the trial). Each plan was communicated to another team of scientists known as the Remote Science Team (RST), meant to be on "Earth", who would analyze the plan and provide feedback, following an artificially imposed six-hour delay meant to resemble what would actually be the case in Mars-Earth communication.

The session was tightly planned in advance with an agenda and links to previously prepared materials. It followed a similar form to earlier meetings, which had also been conducted in the Compendium idea-mapping tool, using the same approach. The main purpose was to develop and capture specific planning items for the next EVA, particularly where the robotic rover was to take photos and how to name those locations, and other aspects of the geologists' planned activities during the EVA. The form of the idea maps was intended to be simple nodes and links following a question-and-answer form. Although one member (Maarten) acted as facilitator and mapper throughout, he was also engaged in the subject matter and aspects of the planning from the perspectives of technical expert and mission team member. He participated fully in most of the discussion, although the two participants were responsible for most of the specifics of the contributed content.

The participants, Brent and Abby, both geologists, were highly engaged throughout the session, both in contributing content, validating how Maarten represented things, making suggestions for new directions, and collaborating on navigation and retrieval of previous material when necessary.

In the transcript that follows, we see some of the key events in a sensemaking episode that occurred during the session. In it, the crew experiences some confusion when they are trying to use a naming convention for locations that the robotic rover will visit to gather samples on the next extra-vehicular activity (EVA). The practitioner, Maarten, mentions to the two participants that he doesn't understand the sample bag naming convention they are using. The participants can't immediately explain it, but they remember that one of them (Brent) had created an explanatory annotation in an idea map some days earlier. In the space of a couple of minutes, the participants and practitioner engage in a collaborative hunt through earlier maps, find the node in question, and place it in the map they'd been working on. Maarten, who was an expert in the software tool being used, employed a number of advanced techniques very rapidly to locate the annotation, aided by comments and feedback from the participants.

The sensemaking episode spans the time from 51:07 to the end of the session at 54:59. It starts as the group is discussing sample bag nomenclature, an unplanned topic that had emerged towards the end of the session. They had already successfully retrieved and transcluded[14] an explanatory node from a previous map that gave the specification for the nomenclature ("letter letter digit digit digit digit") and were beginning to formulate the specific names they wanted to use.

[51:07]

> Brent: "Um well it would be coming up with what we want to use as our letter letters on the, on the site so we can have… like… SF for south face, WF for west face, EF for east face."

> Abby: "OK."

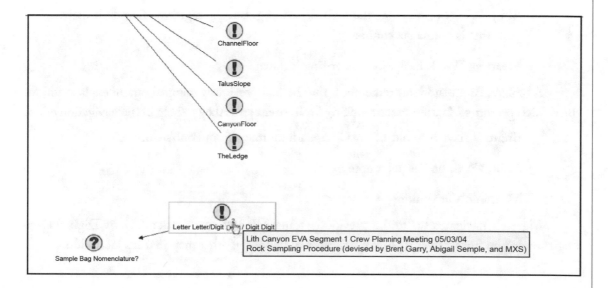

Figure 4.4: Screen at 51:17, showing the explanatory node retrieved from an earlier map.

They proceed with this unproblematically, identifying additional names, until Maarten voices some confusion with the naming approach in general:

> [52:15]

> Maarten: "…I don't understand how you use these, but you do, right? It's letter letter? Is that what it is?"

> Abby: "Yeah. So our sample bag would be, like, S F slash um 2 1 slash zero 1. And that would be, um…"

---

[14] "In computer science, transclusion is the inclusion of a document or part of a document into another document by reference…. The term was coined by hypertext pioneer Ted Nelson in 1963." (http://en.wikipedia.org/wiki/Transclusion). For more on Compendium's transclusion functionality and other hypertext techniques, see http://compendium.open.ac.uk/institute.

In the midst of this Maarten makes an (unprompted) grouping of the nomenclature nodes captured so far, using a Question node:

Maarten: "So this is letter letter right?"

Abby: "Yeah that's all goes there in front of it."

Abby: "And then …"

Maarten: "Alright."

But this grouping does not seem to help completely:

Abby: "OK. So, we know the digit digit thing. But the digit, the first digit digit…. ha… this is gonna get confusing."

Maarten: "Well that's why I'm writing it down."

At 52:59, Brent suddenly remembers that he had previously mapped out an explanation for this, which prompts Maarten to start looking for it. Brent and Abby to help in the navigation effort:

Brent: "I have it in one of my Compendium maps from Pooh's Corner."

Abby: "Yeah he has put a note in."

Maarten: "Oh you do?"

Maarten navigates up to the previously transcluded "Letter Letter / Digit Digit / Digit Digit" node and hovers over its Views indicator to reveal the other map that it's located in:

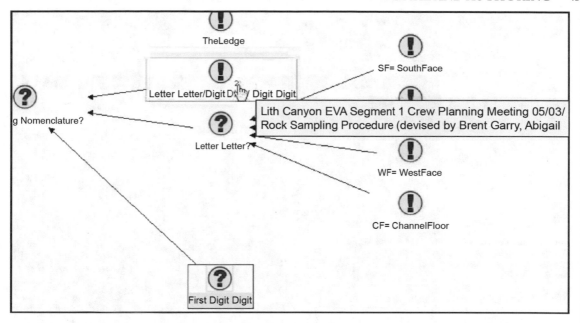

Figure 4.5: Screen at 53:07, showing Maarten hovering over the Views indicator to see which other maps contain the "Letter Letter" node.

He then opens the Views dialog to be able to navigate to that other map and see the node in its original context:

[53:03]

Brent: "I have it as ..."

Abby: "Actually that might be a better..."

Abby: "I think it's that..."

Maarten: "Is it is it the one where, where it's uh..."

Brent: "Could be."

Brent: "Rock sampling procedure..."

Abby: "Yeah."

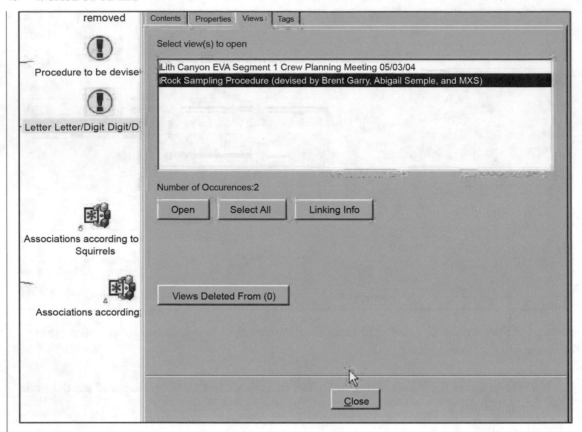

Figure 4.6: Screen at 53:12, showing the Views tab open so as to be able to navigate to the other maps containing the "Letter Letter" node.

Maarten opens this map but that doesn't show the participants what they thought would be there, so they continue to discuss and advise where to look:

[53:12]

Brent: "I thought it was used…"

Abby: "It goes in, yeah, it does it's where it goes into um, it's where it goes into your analysis map is where it is."

Brent: "Yeah I think it's in one of my analysis maps I know that much."

Abby: "If you can find Brent's analysis map it's in there."

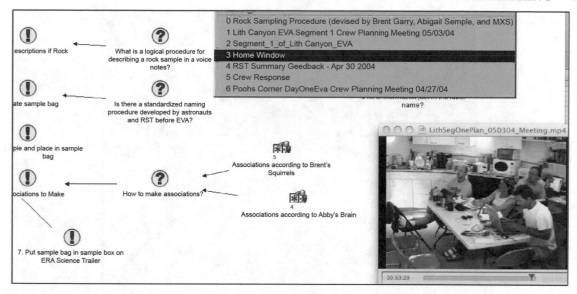

Figure 4.7: Screen and session at 53:29. The crew navigates between maps in search of the explanatory node.

Maarten states, "I find it…" and uses the Window menu to navigate to the Home Window. When he gets there, he finds and opens the "Day_2_of_Poohs_Corner_EVA" map at 53:30.

Within that, he finds and double-clicks on the "Brent's Analysis" map at 53:35. Brent and Abby both indicate it's the right place to look. It takes a while to open due to the large number of photos it contains.

Brent: "Yeah it should be in here."

Abby: "Yeah I think it was it was in there… one of the pictures from your sample bag."

Maarten: "C'mon." [waiting for map to open]

Brent: "There's a lot of photos."

Maarten: "I know."

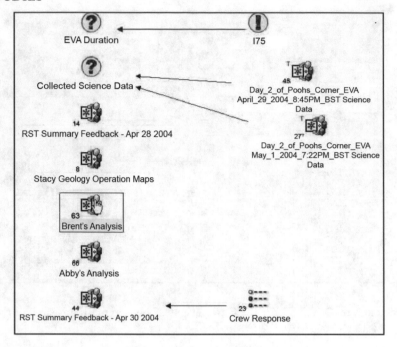

Figure 4.8: Screen at 53:35. Zeroing in on the right maps.

The map opens a few seconds later, but before they can talk about it other members of the team walk in talking about the need to get to another meeting. Maarten deflects them:

Maarten: "Can we do that after we finish this?"

[continued discussion, asking how much more time M needs]

Maarten: "Five more minutes."

[agreement, they leave the room]

00:53:54

Figure 4.9: Maarten deflects an interruption.

With the map open and their attention restored, Brent and Abby direct Maarten to the node of interest. He finds it and Brent points out that the description they need is contained within the detail ("tag" referring to the asterisk detail indicator). Maarten copies the node.

Abby: "We got we got…" [pointing at screen] "go to the left sorry yeah."

Abby: "That one where it says 'note on sample bag naming', the tag in the corner explains."

Brent: "Yeah if you have, if you look at the tag."

Maarten: "OK. I'm just…"

Brent: "OK."

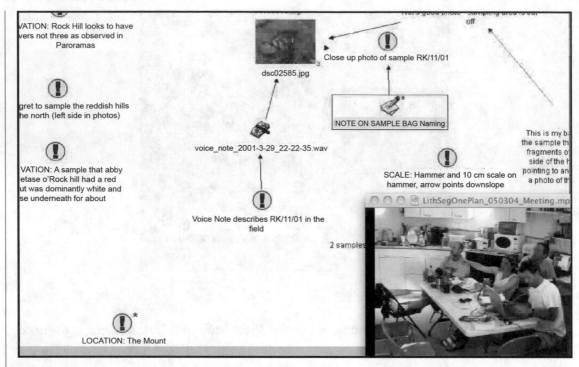

Figure 4.10: Finding the node to copy at 54:14 ("NOTE ON SAMPLE BAG Naming:").

Using the Window menu, Maarten starts to navigate back to the original map to place the transclusion in, but he chooses the wrong meeting map. Abby corrects him and directs him to the right choice on the Window menu.

Abby: "You're in the wrong one. You're in Pooh's Corner."

Maarten: "Of course. So many maps now. Uh…"

Abby: "Uh—down, down, down number five."

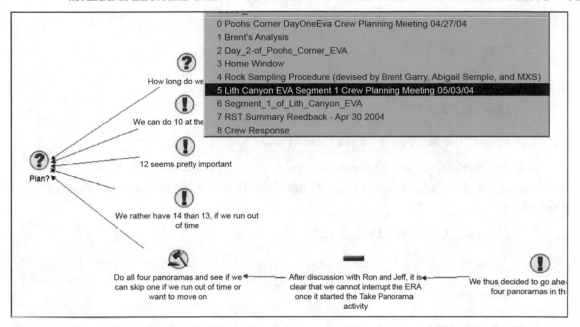

Figure 4.11: Screen at 54:26 (navigating out of the wrong map).

Maarten gets back to the correct map, pastes in the transclusion of the "NOTE ON SAM-PLE BAG Naming:" node, links it to the "Sample Bag Nomenclature" Question, then hovers over the "tag" (asterisk indicator) at Brent's direction to examine the contents:

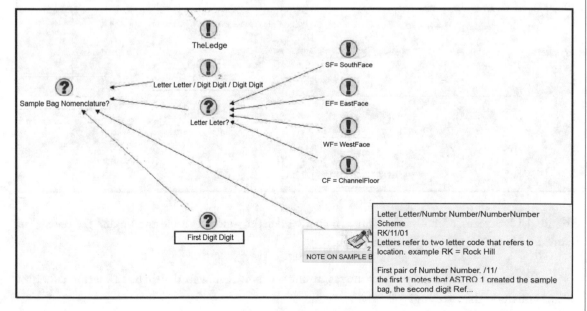

Figure 4.12: Screen at 54:35 after pasting, linking, and hovering.

Brent: "K if you look at the tag…"

Abby: "Yeah."

Brent: "So…"

Maarten: "OK."

Brent: "The letter refers to the location name."

Having established that it's the correct and more complete description, Maarten realizes he can remove the grouping Question node ("First Digit Digit") node he had created earlier (confirmed by Abby):

Maarten: "OK so this I can just…"

Abby: "Yeah."

Maarten: "Delete."

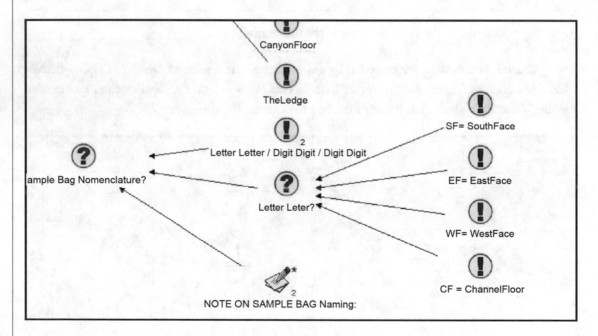

Figure 4.13: Screen at 54:50, final form of map after deleting question node and linking the transcluded node to "Sample Bag Nomenclature."

The team comments on the changes. Brent starts to review in depth, but Maarten cuts him off to conclude the meeting:

Abby: "So that, explains it…"

Brent: "Especially with the tag."

Abby: "That neatly…"

Brent: "The first pair number, the first yeah the first digit in that first pair denotes which astronaut…"

Maarten: "Alright. They can read it. They will get this map. We, uh, we have to shut down so we're gonna end the meeting here, we hope that the RST will have a good meeting."

4.3.1   DISCUSSION

The following narrative threads (among others) were at work in the session:

- performing EVAs, determining and representing what information was needed to perform the upcoming EVA effectively, as well as the best ways to communicate with the RST;

- the ongoing effort to tie together the data, tools, and concepts associated with the Mobile Agents project;

- the unfolding understanding of, and history of previous visits to, the Lith Canyon area;

- the previous meetings of this particular team and the analysis work they had already done;

- an expectation of how Compendium in particular was supposed to function within the project.

The breach in the canonicity of these threads (and the sensemaking trigger for the episode) that occurred was the perception that the "first digit digit" grouping was possibly confusing, and Brent's remembering that he had had an explanation in a previous map from another day. The obstacle was the collective realization that a helpful construct or material pertaining to the subject matter of the exercise was somewhere else, but no one involved immediately remembered where or how to find it. This was a breach in the ability to smoothly create a representation of the EVA in such a way that the RST would be able to follow the map.

The improvised response to this trigger was a spontaneous shift into collaborative navigation to look for the remembered explanatory node, going to a couple of different maps, finding it, agreeing it was the right one, getting back to and placing into the original map, and removing the previous grouping 'first digit digit' node, negotiating and agreeing on the placement of the items, with the outcome that all agreed that the retrieved node resolves the issue and results in a better map and plan for the RST to use.

The character of the interchange instantly shifts to a new one, without the need to stop, analyze, and plan. There is implicit trust on Maarten's part that Brent and Abby will stay engaged and help in suggesting places to look and even in how to navigate among the maps. Similarly, Brent and Abby trust that Maarten will handle the software and data aspects (which he does, accomplishing more than thirty moves in Compendium in the 2 min that comprise the episode).

The very fact that forward movement wasn't stymied shows the collaborative climate that had been built up between practitioner and participants. All were sensitive to the importance of both form and content of the representation and knew, without needing to discuss it, what they could do to help resolve the issue. The team could have just glossed over the naming convention question without addressing it, but their goal (part of the primary narrative) was to create the most useful and engaging map as possible for the RST's use, as well as making links to past work in such a way as to clarify both their present work (the map they were creating in this session) and future work (what the RST and even their own future meetings will encounter—the narrative they were constructing).

The aesthetic and ethical character of the practitioner's actions was already well established at the time of the episode, and did not change in form during the episode. Relationships, roles, and collaborative style all stay intact, even as the three people shift their focus to respond to the challenge presented by the sample bag nomenclature. The aesthetic character of the session was already set in terms of textual refinements, terse node labels, and adhering to a simple tree structure layout for the question and answer nodes. Following, as they did, a simple question-and-answer format, the representations that Maarten constructed in this session appeared to foster dialogicity and openness. This was seen through the conversational style of the meeting and Maarten's demonstrated willingness to be guided and to make changes when requested. The participants were able to suggest new topics and see these incorporated immediately into the representation. The representations were clear and expressive given knowledge of the context and subject matter.

The representation also showed a high degree of textual refinement. The participants and practitioner negotiated, refined, discussed, and revised node labels throughout the session, with all concerned engaged in making sure they got the labels "right." This was fitting since they were creating materials that would be used by other people and systems later on.

The ethical character of the session, consisting of collaborative determination of agenda and topics, discussion and refinement of the textual labels and placement of nodes, consistent requests for validation (even though Maarten acted "unilaterally" in some of his actions), all established a climate where the participants knew that their suggestions or objections would always be listened to. Maarten tacitly balanced the need to proceed efficiently with continual encouragement and solicitation of participant input and validation. He demonstrated the following "values in action" (Friedman, 1996):

- the importance of the mission in the context of the larger space research effort in general and the particular set of related projects that made up the Mobile Agents effort;

- accomplishing the needs and planned agenda within the very tight timeframe, and producing the expected materials with sufficient clarity and quality;

- furthering the research interest in the way the tools were working for the purpose, both individually and together; and

- the "sanctity" of this particular meeting and its video recordings (he defended it from several interruptions from "important" other matters during the course of the session.

As an intact team working in close quarters on a project of high importance to all of them, these values were quite congruent with those of the participants. Maarten's practitioner style created a high degree of collaboration between himself and participants. He "opened up" his conduct of the session so that the work (particularly, but not solely, that concerned with the representation itself) was done in cooperation with the participants, as opposed to non-collaborative approaches such as top-down or directive, practitioner-driven style, or a bottom-up, participant-driven session.

In the next example, we highlight a different kind of improvised collaborative style—this time between a pair of practitioners who had not worked together before.

4.4   EXAMPLE 4: AMES GROUP 4—IMPROVISED TACIT TEAMWORK BETWEEN PRACTITIONERS

The setting was a workshop held at the NASA Ames Research Center where attendees were learning to make better use of an issue mapping technique. Teams were assigned to plan and carry out a 15-min exercise on the theme of space travel, where the only requirement was that the facilitation needed to directly engage participants in the shaping of the issue map, in some way. Some of the sessions went very well, despite that most of the facilitators were relative novices. In most cases, they were able to keep participants directly engaged with the making and editing of the maps throughout their sessions. Some, like the Ames Group 2 session we'll see later on in the chapter, were less successful. In this session, conducted by Ames Group 4, there was a successful outcome.

Figure 4.14: Summary of Ames Group 4 sensemaking episode.

The practitioners, Lena and Sarah, had created a seed map and framed out a simple discussion-mapping exercise. They started off by introducing the context ("identify components of a public education campaign about space") and laid out the ways that they wanted participants to contribute.

The session started with a few pictures and questions and a solicitation on the part of the facilitator, Sarah, for the participants to start contributing ideas. Throughout the session, Sarah constantly related what people were saying to where and how the statements fit onto the map itself, both through verbal statements and by pointing directly at locations on the map. She did not let the conversation swing away from specific contexts represented within the map. Because the participants were so closely engaged, the verbal contributions came in quickly and profusely. A sensemaking episode occurred when the mapper, Lena, who was not very experienced, started to fall behind. But Sarah instantly improvised a method that regulated the flow of conversation as well as Lena's mapping moves, while still weaving both together in such a way that the participant contributions were all integrated coherently onto the map.

The episode was about 2 min long, starting from about halfway through the session. Lena had just captured a participant contribution ("Tell me how I could be an astronaut"), followed by Sarah validating it with the participant.

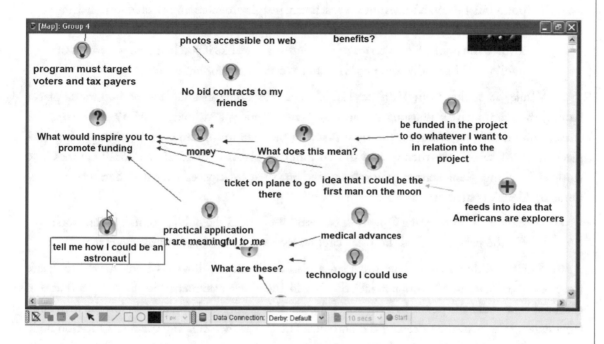

Figure 4.15: Ames Group 4 map at the start of the sensemaking episode

At 14:32, participant Gene made the following contribution:

"Y'know and part of that actually is, is more sort of close interaction like with the people… like I love meeting astronauts, y'know … and I still like meeting astronauts hearing about, hearing their stories and all that."

While Gene was talking, Lena performed some cleanup of the map's layout, and then positioned a new blank node for the next contribution. Sarah noticed that Lena might have missed some of the details, so Sarah provided a helpful reiteration and summary of Gene's statement:

Sarah: **"So close interaction with astronauts …"**

Gene: "Or with the rocket scientists."

Sarah: "Or close interaction with those involved. **Astronauts and rocket scientists, yeah**."

The last bolded point was Sarah's validation as Lena typed the phrase "and rocket scientists", confirming that Lena had captured the point accurately.

The same participant, Gene, then made a fairly long speech (from 15:08 to 15:31):

"I think also sort of one of the underlying things, I don't think it was exactly Jack's point but I think it's relevant here is, is um, people are more uh invested in something if they feel like they are co-creators? Like they're part of it? So if there are ways to involve the public like in terms of decision-making, like if you had contests where the public could actually come up with an advertisement for an example."

While he spoke, from 15:08 to 15:15, Lena was doing cleanup moves in various places around the map, such as adjusting the arrangements of nodes and links. At 15:19 she moved the cursor around as if searching for the right place on the map to capture Gene's point, settling on a place at 15:24, which she then moved to two different places until 15:28. At 15:29 before Gene stopped speaking, Lena started typing "contests" but then backspaced over it as Sarah started re-phrasing Gene's contribution:

Sarah: "So **if we put a Question** that said how could the public become co-creators? Of the program? And then let's capture a couple of your, your ideas about that."

Sarah's subtle guidance here provided a plan for Lena to follow. As Lena started to create the Idea node "contest for commercial", Sarah said the above statement "So if we put a question that said how could the public become co-creators?" This prompted Lena to abandon the Idea node (first erasing the text, then deleting the node itself at 15:37) then creating the new Question node at 15:39 ("How could the public become co-creators of the project?"). Sarah then prompted Lena to create specific Idea nodes in response.

Those actions took from 15:39 through 15:50, while Sarah had already finished the above speech. Then, since the new Question's label displayed below the bottom of the visible map, Sarah provided another narration to guide Lena's actions:

Sarah: "Um… I think … **just move that up a little so we can all see it** and then I think he said what was it? One was a contest for…"

Lena moved her cursor over to the right scrollbar to scroll the map up, while Sarah simultaneously bought her time by explaining to the participants what Lena was doing, and prompting her to create the next set of nodes.

Other participants chimed in in response to these prompts, supplying the content for Lena to create new nodes. Lena herself provided one of these prompts. The sequence ended with Sarah's statement "OK great" which was an acknowledgement that Lena had captured the contributions accurately (depicted in Figure 4.16).

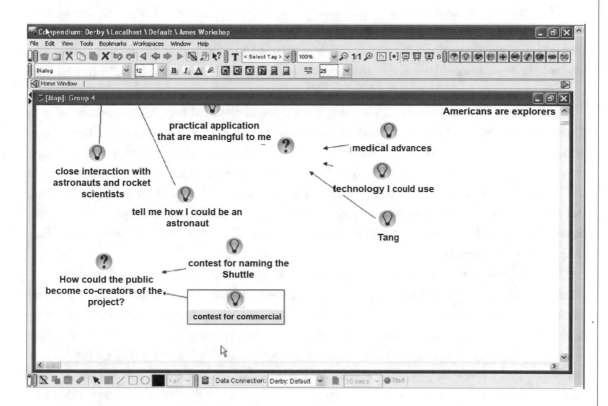

Figure 4.16: Map at conclusion of Ames Group 4 sensemaking episode.

4.4.1   DISCUSSION

Since the setting for the episode was a workshop bringing together people who had not worked together before, there was not the same degree of a priori narrative threads informing the session as in our previous three examples. In this case, the people (including Lena and Sarah) attending the workshop were mainly attending to improve their skills with the Compendium software, as well as to develop the community around that software tool and approach. Within the Ames Group 4 session itself, the primary narrative was the goal of engaging the participants in creating a map fleshing out the discussion of an educational program about the space program. The breach (and sensemaking trigger) that occurred in the episode came when participant Gene's contributions came too quickly for Lena to keep up. The facilitator's (Sarah) response to this was to narrate a strategy for Lena to follow while simultaneously stopping new contributions from coming in—holding forward progress so that the breach could be repaired and progress resumed.

Sarah interrupted Lena's method of capturing the discussion on the map, directing her to create a Question node rather than an Idea, in effect saying *I'm telling you what structure to create. Gene is asking a new question about how could the public become co-creators, so I want you to erase what you were doing and start over.* She directed how the representation should be created and decided what form Gene's contribution should take in the representation, doing this in such a way that elicited further contributions from other participants along the same lines. She did this without spelling out every detail, but making her intention clear by implication.

This action heals the breach. Two people who had not worked together before were able to improvise a facilitative method and pick up each other's cues, all unspoken and in a matter of seconds. They maintained smooth functioning for the session despite their lack of experience working together, and despite their unfamiliarity with the software and equipment (the mapper was not used to a trackpad mouse), and the short time given to plan out the session. The little actions that the Lena and Sarah took were able to keep things on track and preserve the engine of collaboration—where people are actively engaged in looking at, talking about, and modifying or building their shared representations.

Along with sensitivity to participants, effective representational practice is also about sensitivity to the needs and capacities of other practitioners. Effective team practice requires several elements: paying attention to both what the participants are saying; to where, when, and how participant ideas are placed on the representation; and also to where the one's co-practitioner is, how far behind she might be (even in the space of a few seconds). In this example we saw a practitioner perform small moves that helped her co-practitioner catch up, while still keeping participants engaged with the display (and helping to keep the content of the display relevant as well). To be effective with any participatory practice, practitioners have to have a degree of ethical and aesthetic sensitivity. They need to be able to recognize when choices that affect the people they're working with need to be made. Sensitivities and their impact are most easily seen when practitioners encounter a sensemaking challenge—an anomaly in the expected unfolding of events that forces them (however briefly and rapidly) to improvise a response, so that the session can regain progress towards its goals. It's in improvisation that we can most clearly see the character and richness of the action taken, because it is not tied to a prescribed method or script.

In our final example, we will what in effect was a breakdown of collaboration, both between two co-practitioners and between the practitioners and participants.

4.5   EXAMPLE 5: AMES GROUP 2 SESSION—WHEN A SESSION VEERS OFF COURSE

In this example, from the same set of workshop sessions that the Ames Group 4 episode was taken from, we look at an episode where forward progress was not achieved—where there was, in effect, a failure of practitioner sensitivity to participant needs.

Figure 4.17: Ames Group 2 sensemaking episode.

The practitioners had planned a discussion based on a recent newspaper story on "sex in space." They set up a number of opening questions and answers in an issue map, and planned to engage the participants in expanding the discussion they had seeded. One member of the team, Amy, acted as facilitator, and the other as the mapper (Paul). The sensemaking episode we will describe occurred for about 3 min and 44 s of the 15-min session.

To introduce the session, Amy, standing in front of the room, gave a rather lengthy description of the ideas expressed in the map (this intro lasted for more than four and a half minutes, almost a third of the allotted time for the session), but without drawing participant attention directly to the map itself (for example, by pointing at the ideas she was describing). After several minutes of this exposition, she stopped and said, "Now is the time for your contributions," but without providing the participants with a clear method or expectation of how or in what form the contributions should occur.

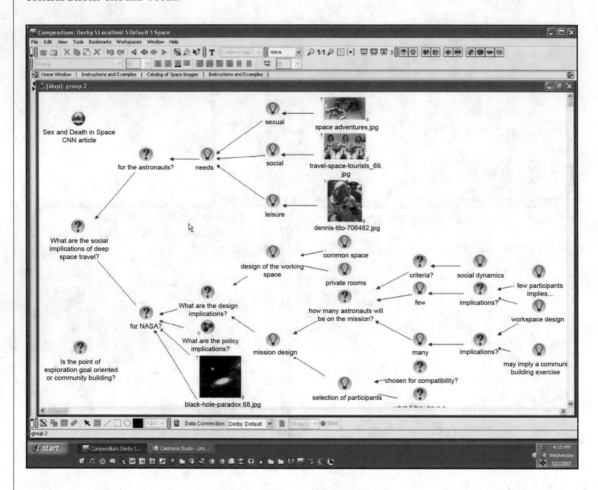

Figure 4.18: Screen at the start of the Ames Group 2 session.

The participants did indeed begin discussing the topic, but not in the way the practitioners had intended. Jed, a participant, raised an objection to the way several of the ideas were mapped in the prepared map. He referred to a specific section (near the top of Figure 4.18) and objected to the way the concepts "sexual" and "leisure" as needs were shown in the map, stating, "They don't belong separate in, in my view...." Several other participants joined in, saying that they did or didn't agree with the objections, all referring specifically to how the ideas appeared on the prepared map.

During this conversation, Amy made tentative verbal interventions once or twice. She commented on the subject matter being discussed, again without directly referring to the actual map, and tried to draw the discussion into the intended fleshing-out of the prepared map ("So do you think that there are some other kind of leisure that can be considered part of …"). The participants, however, continued to discuss the specific map area and whether or not it was a good representation, also making suggestions for augmenting the mapped concepts in that area ("You know, you might as well add psychological needs"). In the meantime, Paul did some mapping of the discussion, again without engaging participants or directing their attention to the map.

After several minutes, Paul attempted to intervene to try to get the session back on track. He stopped the discussion and highlighted an area on the map that the participants were referring to. He acknowledged that the points they were making could be reflected and expanded on in the map—but that he wasn't going to. Instead, he asked them to look elsewhere on the map for the specific questions he wanted them to respond to:

> "I think that all of those are points well taken and can be, you can massage this section up here… but the section up here is really driving the true point for us which is down here [he used the cursor to point at the lower section of the map]. What are the implications for NASA and how they design everything else? So yes I agree with all of those points up here, there could be more needs, these things could be grouped underneath one another, and stuff like that. Um but where we were going with that was, all of this stuff down here, and what are the social dynamics of, say, what are the implications of having just a few people on a spacecraft versus having many. How does that impact not only the design of the mission, are you trying to do a community-building thing out in space somewhere. Um, and what are the implications of too few participants off in space for four years."

While saying this, he uses the cursor to point at and circle the areas of the map he wants the participants to focus on.

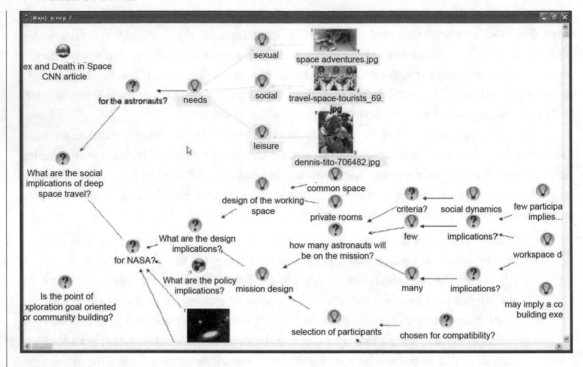

Figure 4.19: Screen showing Paul's highlighting of the area he didn't want participants to focus on.

As soon as he finishes his statement, Amy attempted again to intervene ("Yeah so …") but is interrupted by another participant, Mark, who took the discussion off in yet another direction. The session continued, but there were no more attempts by participants to engage with or influence the form or content of the map itself. Instead, the session becomes a more typical discussion, without paying attention to the map or even looking at it to see if their comments were being reflected on it.

4.5.1   DISCUSSION

The sensemaking trigger for the episode came when several participants objected to the way the prepared map was structured and wanted to discuss it. For the practitioners, this caused a disconnect with the representational structure they had set up, as well as to their intended process and plan for the session. The incoming participant input didn't fit the structure. For Amy and Paul, this caused the session to veer off course.

The two practitioners differed in their approaches to try to get the session back on track. Amy tried to discuss the issues participants were bringing up in terms of the subject matter (although not using the map's structure), while Paul pointed to the area of the map the participants were discussing and, while acknowledging their issues could be valid, directed participants to "all this stuff down here" that was the intended focus. By doing this, Amy and Paul made the implicit choice to hold off their mapping efforts until the discussion took the form they had intended, rather than (for example) trying to adapt to it, or reflect this different direction on the map itself.

Neither approach had the desired outcome. The participants ignored Paul's direction (as well as Amy's comments) and went off in another direction, continuing to discuss the general topic but without reference to the map itself. The discussion and representation diverged from each other, with the participants no longer referring to the representation. After Paul's attempt, neither Amy nor Paul made further attempts to re-engage the participants with the representation.

Amy's and Paul's actions could be thought of in terms of displaying insufficient ethical sensitivity to the needs of their participants in this specific session (although the same actions might well have been effective in another context). Their moves and interventions were not well adapted to the ways the participants were taking the discussion. None of their moves were attuned enough to achieve the desired form of representational engagement.

Let's compare these actions to those of Lena and Sarah in Ames Group 4. Even though their level of practitioner experience and mapping skills was similar to those for Amy and Paul, Lena and Sarah's level of sensitivity to participant needs and sensibilities was higher. The ways that they cared for and responded to these needs was effective. They were able to "roll with the punches" and absorb rapid participant input, finding ways to represent the input and the map and get the participants to validate and help shape the representation, and to let Lena catch up when she got behind.

In Amy and Paul's session, it is a bit ironic is that their participants did, in fact, start off the session by attempting to directly engage with the map. However, this mode of engagement (critiquing the way it had been arranged) did not accord with what the practitioners had intended. Amy and Paul were "tone deaf" in the sense that they did not respect the direction participants were trying to go, but also without making the practitioners' desired direction clear (and inviting) enough for participants to follow. Paul did make a strong attempt to correct the course of the session—even using the representation itself—but it did not have sufficient sensitivity to participant sensibilities at that moment. In effect, it denied the direction the participants wanted to go, but without providing a clear or inviting path for them to participate in the intended way.

It's not that the practitioner choices were bad or wrong in any absolute sense, but rather that they did not result in productive engagement with and further development of the representation in this particular session, in effect preventing the representation from playing a meaningful role for the participants.

4.6   SUMMARY

In this chapter, we reviewed practitioner sensemaking and improvisation in five diverse kinds of participatory representational sessions.

Tom and Jackie

- Situation: Parent and child interaction over explaining how to use a compass.

- Sensemaking moment: Child comes to mother, upset because he can't understand how to use his new compass.

- Practitioner response: Mother improvises a representational game to teach him how.

Hab crew

- Situation: Science team constructing a plan for a robotic geological exploration.

- Sensemaking moment: Realization that needed explanatory material is elsewhere and must be found.

- Practitioner response: Collective improvised search to find and place the missing reference material.

Contingency Planning

- Situation: Ad hoc team conducting a risk assessment exercise to create a business contingency plan.

- Sensemaking moment: Participant grabs the "floor" and starts directing the practitioner how to draw the map.

- Practitioner response: Practitioner changes style from directive to supportive and lets the participant run the show.

Ames Group 4

- Situation: Workshop team facilitating issue-mapping discussion on topic of public education on space program.

- Sensemaking moment: Participant input comes in too fast for idea mapper to capture it in the representation.

- Practitioner response: Facilitator improvises a method to slow down the input and allow mapper to catch up.

Ames Group 2

- Situation: Workshop team facilitating issue-mapping discussion on topic of "sex in space."

- Sensemaking moment: Discussion veers off intended course.

- Practitioner response: Attempts to correct by pointing to where on the map the intended discussion should be happening.

Like a basketball game, the success of a participatory representational session is not decided in a single moment, but is the aggregation of many moves and choices. What the diversity in the case studies in this chapter has shown is that effective representational practice is not a matter of a particular style or method of representation. The five examples exhibited a wide variety of skills, styles, tool use, and session characteristics. In each, we explained why a particular style, medium, and facilitative approach (whether formal or informal) was in use, and that some sort of challenge, obstacle, or anomaly intruded, posing a possible interruption to the progress of session (even if a temporary one), followed by improvised actions on the part of someone playing a facilitative role, with various consequences to the session as a whole. Seen from outside the context of a specific session, these are not dramatic events. Within a session, however, from the perspective of a practitioner trying to achieve coherence, engagement, and usefulness for the participants and the session's goals, such moments often make the difference between success and something less.

By highlighting episodes where practitioner improvisation took place, we are not saying that there's always improvisation in participatory representational sessions. Sometimes practitioners stick to established techniques and procedures throughout a session, and often those can be effective within themselves. Through observations of hundreds of sessions using many different types of representational approaches we have seen that there is nearly always practitioner sensemaking of some kind, even if brief. Unexpected obstacles, challenges, or anomalies arise. Often, an improvised response is the best, or even only, way of addressing these triggers. As we will discuss in more depth below, there are always primary and inner narratives informing any session, both "lived-in" and shaped narratives. Any activity involving representations involves aesthetics and choices about how to shape the artifacts. And any actions that one takes as a practitioner that affects participants and others always have an ethical dimension, even if one is simply following a pre-established process.

4.6.1 MULTIPLE NARRATIVES

We all live in multiple, simultaneous narratives. What we call the "narrative framing" for any event or episode is never singular, even if some narratives may be more in the background at particular times. What is most salient at any given moment depends on the particular situation and its imperatives. One narrative can suddenly impinge on another, or they can even merge.

In the Tom and Jackie episode, there is the narrative of Tom as a happy little boy at home on a weekend, whose parents have just given him a gift; for Jackie, there was the "immediate" narrative of her usual set of weekend tasks and time spent with family and a visiting friend, pottering about the kitchen while the children rocketed around on various activities. There were also a whole gamut of larger, long-lived narratives, such as being an effective, loving parent that teaches her children the life skills they need to be self-reliant, but with the knowledge that their parents are always there loving and supporting them.

For the Hab crew, some of the many intersecting narratives at work were the enveloping Mobile Agents project, having to do with using new e-science tools for scientific collaboration on space missions, proving them out in a field trial; the ongoing story of learning how best to collaborate with another science team with whom they were not in direct, simultaneous communication; the specific histories of the geological explorations of the surrounding area and previous EVAs; the evolution of the specific set of maps that the teams had been building (hence the value placed on finding and embedding the explanatory naming convention node); the evolution of the methods for doing the geological explorations themselves (hence the significance of getting good explanations for why they were making the particular naming convention recommendation at that time; the pressures of the project on that day (hence the need to wall off this one hour of activity and defend it from other team members who wanted to interrupt the mapping session for other reasons; and the various career and individual interests and trajectories of the crew members.

When a participatory representational exercise occurs, it is all about *producing* an artifact that has its own narrative coherence; a created narrative, embodied in an artifact, telling a story that (hopefully) others can read and understand. Lived-in narratives are sometimes shared and sometimes individual; sometimes fragmented, and sometimes richly coherent (moments when everything seems to be related). The point for the analyst is that to understand the significance and effectives of an improvised action, it must be placed in enough of a narrative context to make its significance clear—not that it "just happened." This gives us the means to understand how aesthetic and ethical choices have led to particular outcomes, which themselves are often multiple in nature. For Tom and Jackie, these outcomes included that now Tom could use the compass and understand it; Jackie had taught him something, and they enjoyed the experience together. For the Hab crew, outcomes included that they finished their planning exercise, and the map recording it, on schedule; that their map had tight forward and backward hypertextual links to past and future actions; and that the team had created a more rich and useful reference tool for other teams than they might have done otherwise.

4.6.2   LOOKING AT INSTANCES OF PRACTICE IN EXPERIENTIAL TERMS

How does it help to look at examples of participatory representational practice in this way? Our goal throughout this book has been to make clear exactly what the contribution of a participatory representational practitioner is. What do people acting in this role decide to do or not to do? We want to illuminate the values in action they are demonstrating, and how those are responsive to the participants, situation, and stakeholders (ethics); the skills with which they able to create (or help to be created) a coherent, engaging, and useful representation, and why it is meaningful and expressive for its intended audience (aesthetics); the character and quality of the situation they are in, and the intended arc of events and what sorts of breaches of expectations occur (the primary narrative) as well as what is the story they are trying to create (the produced narrative); the specific nature of the anomalies they encounter and how exactly those disrupt (even if temporarily) forward movement (sensemaking) in such a way that they must (even if temporarily) abandon their assumed procedures; and what fresh, creative, unplanned actions they take (improvisation) in order to overcome the obstacles and resume moving forward toward their goals.

This is important in order to more clearly be able to articulate the kinds of sensemaking challenges that can occur, as well as the kinds of aesthetic, improvisational, and narrative skills that might be necessary to acquire and develop in order to fluidly address sensemaking challenges, as well as the ethical dimensions and considerations to be aware of and sensitive to. Such considerations **always** pervade our actions as participatory practitioners. While all of these can be discussed in the abstract as principles, real practice doesn't consist solely of the application of abstract principles. It happens too fast, and too contextually specific for abstractions to be of much use in and of themselves. By looking at fluid (and not-so-fluid) practice in "slow motion," as we have tried to do in this chapter, we can better see what small actions really took place, what differences they made, and their significance in experiential terms.

Looking at participatory representational practice in this way gives us handles to talk about what would otherwise be a blur of activity. It shows the richness of the experiential dimensions at work, and how choices and moves in the improvised process can matter (as well as what choices might have had very different outcomes). It lets us "replay" a session with appreciation for the nuances of what actually made it work. In actual practice it is often these unplanned moments, where things go off the rails, where how we handle them as practitioners makes the difference in how we are effective—or not—in achieving participant engagement. It's such engagement which makes the difference in achieving successful outcomes reflecting actual participation. It can help us see where opportunities lie to achieve Knowledge Art in our participatory practices, as we glimpsed in many of the sessions analyzed in this chapter.

In our concluding chapter, we discuss some implications of this approach.

CHAPTER 5

Discussion and Conclusions

In Chapter 3, we discussed Schön's call for an *epistemology of artistry in professional practice*, a theme that has informed our work on participatory representational practice since its inception. While giving many examples of how practitioners as diverse as architects, musicians, and urban planners explored and develop their expertise in their chosen fields, Schön also felt he was just scratching the surface:

> We know very little about the ways in which individuals develop the feel for media, language, and repertoire which shapes their reflection-in-action. This is an intriguing and promising topic for future research. (1983: 271-2)

In this book, we've attempted to provide concepts and methods to describe participatory representational practice in such a way as to highlight the actual experience of such practices. As Schön encouraged, we want to better understand what practitioners confront and overcome through their skills, creativity, and responsiveness to others. We first discussed how Knowledge Cartography is a key strategy for collective intelligence in the face of complexity, and the need to understand the human skillset involved in engaging people in such representations. Chapter 2 then turned to the ways this subject has been treated in the HCI literature on Participatory Design, describing how the research has generally not given sufficient focus to the moves and choices that practitioners make in the moment-to-moment conduct of their sessions, although many researchers have called for better understanding in this area. Then, in Chapter 3, we outlined a conceptual framework for characterizing such actions according to the facets of Knowledge Art, discussing how the experiential dimensions of aesthetics, ethics, narrative, sensemaking, and improvisation provide key perspectives from which to observe participatory representational practice. Finally, in Chapter 4, we brought these concepts to life by applying them to five different case studies of actual practice.

Throughout, the questions that have occupied us are: How do people actually engage others in creating participatory representations? What kinds of choices and actions take place? Answering these is not simply a matter of techniques, tools, and processes, though they can certainly help. In real situations with real people, sometimes techniques can stultify, or are not the right match for a situation, or require creative human intervention to make them really work. In this book we have sought to provide a language for talking about these actions, the practitioner choices behind them, and their experiential dimensions.

We'll now examine some implications for the practice of fostering participant engagement and the PD research agenda, and link these considerations to efforts to inculcate dispositions for "21st Century competencies" for education.

5.1   FOSTERING ENGAGEMENT AND EFFECTIVE PD PRACTICE

In Chapter 1, we argued that improving our capacity for collective intelligence through the use of such representational forms as knowledge maps and concept structures requires enhancing the human skillsets involved. We then focused on the ways that participatory representational practitioners can help participants engage with such representations by looking closely on the moment-to-moment choices practitioners make, which we analyzed in experiential terms. This approach sheds light on a number of themes that can help PD become the "fully professional practice" that Bødker and Iversen called for (2002). As Schön argued, improving professional practice calls for self-reflection as much as it does improved tools and techniques. In Chapter 3, we saw the need for PD research to place aesthetic and ethical concerns into the foreground, and to better examine how PD practitioners deal with unexpected turns of events in the unfolding of sessions and projects. We saw calls for more emphasis on PD's facilitative aspect, especially its performative and interactional aspects. Conceptions of facilitation that rest on notions of "objectivity" and "neutrality," with their connotations of that practitioners can somehow stay outside the fray, do not provide enough insight into the inevitability of intervention and the need to understand what informs the moves that practitioner can, do, and must make. When representations are involved, as they nearly always are in PD efforts, practitioners must watch for and help guide how participants engage with the representations, as well as how their own actions either foster or inhibit such engagement. Effective participatory representational practice means making judicious choices in the heat of the moment, guided by an understanding of the stories surrounding and being constructed by participants. It involves sensitivity to the aesthetic and ethical considerations at work in the situation, and quick thinking when anomalies and setbacks are encountered. In Chapter 4, we saw a number of instances of such choices, and took a close look at the experiential dimensions at play in the practitioners' actions.

Some PD practitioners (like some athletes or musicians) seem to be naturally talented at working with participants, while others develop skills and sensitivities over time, through combinations of coaching, practice, and tool support. Still others seem at times to be obtuse or tone-deaf to participant needs, even though they may be highly capable in other areas. There's no recipe for being good at this, just as there's no recipe for being an effective musician, athlete, writer, or conversationalist. It's not simply about the ability to make intrusive interventions, though sometimes those are what are needed. Sometimes the most effective strategy is to just set the stage and then let participants run with the representation-making (as we saw in the Contingency Planning episode). Sometimes it's a direct side-by-side partnership, as in the Hab example. Sometimes there is a lot of handholding needed, and sometimes effective practice requires more of a virtuosic solo or duo performance (as in the Ames Group 4 example, where sensitivity to the needs and capacities of other practitioners as well as to participants made the difference). Effective moves and sensitivity also does not mean "rolling over" (though sometimes, acquiescence can be the right move, as it was for the Contingency Planning episode). It is possible to be assertive and even controlling, and still be effective in fostering engagement, as we saw in the Tom and Jackie and Hab Crew episodes.

We have argued for the need to attend to the people who are effective in these practices, and learn from them (and instructively, from those who are less fluent). We have argued that what we call Participatory Representational Practice is a poorly understood but vital new civic skill for all types of collaborative knowledge work, where the complexity of the problem requires, or benefits from, the construction of a collectively owned representational artifact—whether scribbled on a napkin or detailed in a multiuser computational modeling tool. Hence, this includes meeting facilitators, but extends to many others, such as students, teachers, designers, academics and policy analysts.

Using the concepts we've described in this book foregrounds such considerations for discussion and reflection by practitioners and researchers. Applying these concepts can deepen understanding of the nature of professional practice, enabling practitioners and researchers to see, discuss, and reflect on the ways in which the aesthetic and ethical aspects of their practices intertwine. Such an approach can be used by PD researchers and practitioners to learn how to "read" the moment-to-moment activities in a session, for the elements of practitioner experience in crafting representations and responding to participants and others. It can be used to identify, diagnose, and reflect on individual choices and moves *in situ*. It can help both novice and experienced practitioners to become more intentional and reflective in their practices, enabling them to become more participant-centered, and to both ask and solicit more "higher-ordered" questions (Sawyer, 2004: 18). Unlike segregated methods that focus on individual tools and techniques, what we are doing is raising awareness of what is constant in the practitioner experience regardless of the particular approach employed. The considerations in this book can help provide a reflective model that individual practitioners, practitioners in peer groups, and coaches and trainers of practitioners can apply regardless of specific context.

Throughout its history, PD researchers and practitioners have aspired to improve the ability of the people most affected by a technological, organizational, or social change to directly participate in the design of solutions, rather than having them imposed from above. Effective participation, as well as effective practice, rests in large part on the competence and willingness to engage on the part of the workers and community members that take part in a PD effort. Bringing participative skills to the forefront for a larger proportion of the population requires these abilities to be recognized and fostered within our educational systems. It is here that we turn to our concluding section.

5.2   LEARNING AND EDUCATION

Dispositions are now at least as important as knowledge and skills… how we approach problems … radically contingent on context… in the moment … in the situation, and how we respond. Dispositions cannot be taught. They can only be cultivated. (John Seely Brown, 2013)[15]

It's more than knowledge and skills. For the innovation economy, dispositions come into play: readiness to collaborate; attention to multiple perspectives; initiative; persistence; curiosity. While the content of a learning experience is important, the particular content is irrelevant. What really matters is how students react to it, shape it, or apply it. The purpose of learning in the 21st century is not to recite inert knowledge but to transform it. It's time to change the subject. (Larry Rosenstock, 2013)[16]

As we bring this book to a close, we wish to establish the important connection between the skills and dispositions we have documented in professional workplace contexts, and the ways in which we prepare the next generation for this. So let us turn our attention to the world of education.

A society's capacity to learn is central to its wellbeing. The turbulence of today's social and economic conditions places unprecedented pressure on people's capacity to deal with uncertainty and adapt to change. The personal and collective inability to cope—far less thrive—when stretched and challenged becomes a profound problem for society when it results in widespread personal disengagement from school, employment and community. In what is forecast to be a very challenging socio-economic near-term future, a profound challenge for the education system is the nurturing of personal qualities and skillsets that equip citizens for challenge and change—from children and young people onwards into adult life, to the workforce.

A global network of researchers and practitioners uses the shorthand term "21st century competencies" (21CC) to capture the expansion of education beyond traditional curriculum focusing on the mastery of discipline-specific knowledge and skills (also referred to as 21st century skills and learning-to-learn, each with their own nuances, communities and debates). Numerous websites emphasize the employability and economic implications of creating graduates with such transferable skills.

What is meant by this shorthand? A 2012 review by the Canadian National Council on Measurement in Education and Pearson identified critical thinking, creativity, collaboration, metacognition, and motivation (Lai and Viering, 2012). The US National Research Council (National Research Council, 2011) identified cognitive skills (nonroutine problem solving, systems thinking

---

[15] Invited address to U.S. Department of Education reimaginingeducation.org conference. This specific quote: http://www.c-spanvideo.org/clip/4457327.

[16] LearningREimagined project: http://learning-reimagined.com. Larry Rosenstock: http://audioboo.fm/boos/1669375-50-seconds-of-larry-rosenstock-ceo-of-hightechhigh-on-how-he-would-re-imagine-learning.

and critical thinking), interpersonal skills (ranging from active listening, to presentation skills, to conflict resolution), and intrapersonal skills, which are personal qualities that equip a learner (broadly clustered under adaptability and self-management/self-development). A large international academic and industrial project called The Assessment and Teaching of 21st Century Skills (ATC21S, 2012) is under way, using a classification of Knowledge, Skills, and Attitudes, Values and Ethics (atc21s.org). The first book from this project provides a comprehensive introduction to methodological and technological issues around 21CC assessment, with a taxonomy distilled from the literature as follows: Ways of Thinking, Ways of Working, Tools for Working and Living in the World. This survey included the European framework for key competencies (European Commission, 2006), and the OECD-CERI analyses of "new millennial learners" (OECD, 2001). Deakin Crick has provided academic reviews of the field (Deakin Crick, 2012; Deakin Crick, et al. 2014).

The educational debate sometimes risks polarization, with those who champion more traditional curriculum and examinations seeing a focus on transferable competencies as a distraction from real education. However, a more balanced view is that "competencies" can only be developed meaningfully in the context of "content," while "content" becomes far more engaging and meaningful when learners can exercise the different "competencies."

The quotes opening this section talk specifically about not skills but *dispositions*. The work in this field emphasizes that just about the only thing we can be sure the future holds is more turbulence. An education system fit for our times must help build the qualities that citizens require to cope, even thrive, amidst constant change, with an appetite for new kinds of problems, and an orientation to strategic personal and collective sensemaking that is suited to tackling these. In our prior work (Buckingham Shum and Deakin Crick, 2012), we distilled some of the theoretical background to educational research into learning dispositions, and describe the results of more than 10 years of research to develop an assessment technique which serves as a form of "dispositional learning analytics"—a way to being to quantify this quality. To illustrate just two of the seven key dispositions identified in this work, consider resilience and meaning-making.

- **Resilience:** In a society where it will be increasingly the norm to confront novel dilemmas, this is a vital quality. Resilient learners are "up for a challenge" which takes them out of their comfort zone. They persevere when others might give up, because they know that this is when deeper learning can take place. The opposite pole is dependence and fragility: learners are risk-averse, and more easily go to pieces when they get stuck or make mistakes. This disposition echoes the influential work of Dweck on fixed versus growth "mindsets" (Dweck, 1999).

- **Meaning Making:** A complex society, with many interacting systems, needs learners, citizens and a workforce with the capacity to see connections between what one is learning and what one already knows. The ability to see connections and narrative amidst hyperconnectivity and conflicting perspectives, is a scarce, much sought after ability.

What we are proposing, therefore, is a convergence between two important strands. We have on the one hand this growing body of work into 21st century competencies, and specifically into learning dispositions—not just from academic researchers, but many practitioners in the trenches—arguing that young people (and indeed citizens at large, and specifically workforces) need a new transferable set of qualities that equips them for the novel challenges and complexity of society. These qualities can be seen to come together in what we have called Knowledge Art in this book. Knowledge Art is quite an advanced mix of dispositions and skills, which we have sought to articulate here for the first time. The resonances between the two strands are, we suggest, striking. The educational work on 21st century competencies already shows that these can be nurtured intentionally by schools in primary age children. Just as this book has sought to provide a missing language for an important professional practice, a language for dispositions such as "learning power" provides a vocabulary which was missing for students and teachers to talk about dispositions (Claxton, 1999; Deakin Crick, 2006, 2007).

This convergence opens up the intriguing question of how early we could begin to nurture Knowledge Art in our young people. It is well within the abilities of older teenagers to facilitate a team discussion with appropriate visuals, but nobody has ever sought to make this an explicit object of reflection, or part of the formative assessment of the individual or group's performance. Until now, we lacked Schön's "epistemology," a set of rubrics, which would provide some principled basis for reflection and feedback. With an initial version now articulated, we invite colleagues who see the potential to work with us in piloting this in schools, as part of our broader ambition to see this work translate into practitioner training resources.

The fact that these are undoubtedly more complex qualities to assess than those measured in traditional exams is, for us, not a reason to abandon such an effort, but another brick in the wall of evidence that assessment regimes must evolve, to equip an educational system fit for purpose for our times. It is fundamentally a question of whether education systems will continue to value only what can be counted easily at scale, rather than devising new ways to count what we really should value. Learning analytics—the use of computational data and analysis techniques in education—may offer one helping hand (Buckingham Shum, 2012). As it becomes increasingly possible to log the interactions between people, and their use of digital representations, to make sense of natural language and to parse graphical representations, new possibilities open for mining and formalizing patterns of interest in massive datasets. The formative assessment tools described in the Appendix, developed from the conceptual and practical foundations described in Chapters 2–4, could provide the basis for quantifying, in ways that are computationally tractable, what goes on in collective sensemaking. Future work should investigate to what extent the analytical representations we have created manually might be generated automatically as visual analytics, providing insight for participants and coaches on participatory representational practice.

Looking forward, our intent is to translate the analytical tools and concepts we have described into instruments for coaching diagnostics, that can be applied to professional groups, consulting practices, and in schools and colleges where the personal qualities and skills required to be a Knowledge Artist can begin to be nurtured in the next generation.

CHAPTER 6

Appendix: Knowledge Art Analytics

In this Appendix, we present five analytical tools that can be used to help surface the kinds of considerations discussed in the previous chapters when considering instances of participatory representational practice. Each tool is discussed individually in terms of its motivation, structure, and artifacts produced. [17]

The tools, when used together, comprise a method for producing an analytical "dossier" for instances of practice, examining it from several different experiential and practical perspectives. The tools help produce the kinds of analysis used in Chapter 4. They are summarized in the table below.

Table 6.1: Analysis tools

Analytical Tool	Description
Shaping form	Characterizing the representational character of a whole session to delineate the intended and actual shaping that took place
Coherence, Engagement, and Usefulness (CEU) analysis	Mapping the coherence, engagement, and usefulness dimensions of timeslots within the session. Aids in identifying sensemaking episodes
Sensemaking Episode description	Rich description of a sensemaking episode, including triggers, dialogue and descriptions of events
Moves and Choices analysis	Micro-moment moves and choices during a sensemaking episode
Framing analysis	Characterizing the practitioner actions during a sensemaking episode in aesthetic, ethical, and experiential terms

Generally, the analytical instruments described in the following sections are applied in the sequence represented in Figure 6.1.[18] The aim in following this set sequence is to achieve both qualitative triangulation (Fortner and Christians, 1981) and increasing theoretical sensitivity (Strauss

---

[17] For more on these tools, see Selvin, 2011. Examples of each kind of analysis can be found at http://people.kmi.open.ac.uk/selvin/analysis/.

[18] Note that "transcript" is included as one of the steps in an analysis sequence. Developing a transcript of a complete episode is really an analysis tool in and of itself, since it requires paying close attention to what is said and done in a session and begins the process of sensitizing the analyst to the nuances of actions, statements, characters, and context. However, there is certainly nothing new about developing a transcript, so we did not include it in our descriptions of analysis tools below. There are many fine guides to developing transcripts, such as Bailey, 2008.

and Corbin, 1990) by looking at the data through multiple lenses. While the following discussion assumes that the tools are being applied to recordings (screen, video, audio) of a session of practice, they can also be applied to a live event with careful attention and good note-taking.

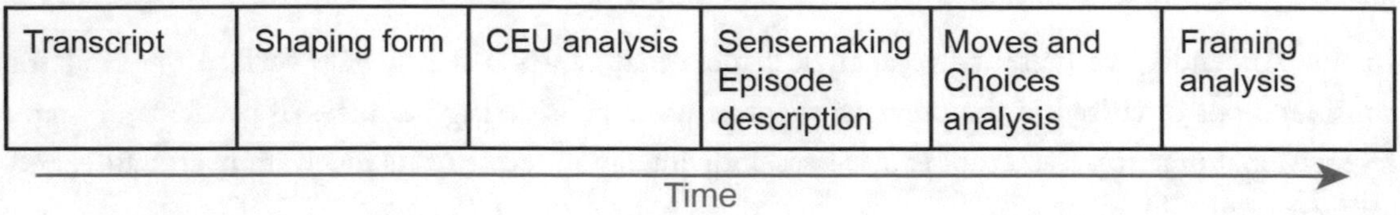

Transcript	Shaping form	CEU analysis	Sensemaking Episode description	Moves and Choices analysis	Framing analysis

Time ⟶

Figure 6.1: Analysis sequence.

6.1   SHAPING FORM

The Shaping Form comprises a set of questions asked about an instance of practice (for example, a facilitated meeting or session) as a whole. It aims at characterizing the representational character of the session. It describes what kinds of roles participants and practitioners played in the shaping of the representation, both as a result of planning and intention, and in response to whatever exigencies actually occurred during the session.

The questions included a characterization of the overall ecosystem of the session (the surrounding context, purpose of the session, types of participants), as well as a number of questions designed to put focus on the interaction of people with the representation. Table 6.2 relates the questions to the dimensions of the framework in Section 3.3.

Table 6.2: Relation of Shaping Form questions to conceptual framework	
Shaping form question	**Relation to conceptual framework (section 0)**
What shaping was intended (how the session was planned to work, what shaping the planners intended to occur, and how it would be accomplished)?	Shaping itself is largely the province of aesthetics [**p**], the construction of meaningful form. This question refers to the planned or intended sorts of shaping (which may or may not have occurred in the actual session).
What was the level and quality of participant and practitioner engagement (with maps, subject matter, process, environment)?	This question concerns the relationships of participants, practitioners, and representation to each other [framework elements **d, e, f, g**], as well as to the surrounding context and resources [**i, j**].

What types of shaping actually occurred during the session?	Means to report what sorts of aesthetic shaping [p] took place in the actual session.
If the intended shaping went awry, why did that occur? What blocks an intended shaping? How are the blocks resolved or avoided?	Identifies what sensemaking [s] triggers may have occurred, placing them in the context of the overall narrative trajectory of the session [r]. Explores the degree of improvisation [t] in resolving or avoiding obstacles to progress.
Who did the shaping, for what reasons? What contributions to the shaping occurred?	Maps the shaping actions [p] onto the way their performers related to the representation [d, f].
How were decisions about shaping made? What kinds of decisions were they? Who made them, on what basis? How were these decisions taken up into the representation itself (if they are)? Which are ignored or dropped? Why?	Looks at the choice making involved in both shaping actions and participant inclusion or exclusion in those actions. Often the clearest way to discern the situational ethics [q] of the practitioners.

The result takes the form of the document shown in Figure 6.2.

If the intended shaping ran off the rails, why did that occur?

> There was no significant running off the rails in this session. Even when the mapper got slightly behind, the facilitator made sure that she provided (or asked again for) material that hadn't been captured. The map was slightly messy by the end, but coherent (well-formed questions, links, and answers).

Who did the shaping, for what reasons? What contributions to the shaping occurred?

> The facilitator and mapper managed the map shaping itself for the most part. Participants contributed ideas verbally throughout but did not question or suggest shaping moves (they appeared to readily accept how the shaping was done). Most participant refinements were verbal rather than map-oriented.

How were decisions about shaping made? What kinds of decisions were they? Who made them, on what basis?

How were these decisions taken up into the representation itself (if they are)?

> See previous. As mentioned above it appeared almost as if the mapper and facilitator had rehearsed and agreed how they would work together. They presented what would look to a newcomer as a nearly seamless front, with the facilitator appearing to prompt the mapper's actions (that she had in fact already started in most cases (e.g. "We're just adjusting the map so we can get a little more space here")), sometimes suggesting that something should be captured differently (e.g. as a question with hanging answers).

Figure 6.2: Portion of the Ames Group 4 session's Shaping Form.

With the overall character of the representational role described in the Shaping form, the CEU tool is next used to zoom into a lower level of detail to characterize the session as it unfolded over time.

6.2   COHERENCE, ENGAGEMENT, AND USEFULNESS (CEU) ANALYSIS

Coherence, engagement, and usefulness are normative imperatives that a participatory representational practitioner should follow in any session.

- Keeping the representation, and the interaction of participants with it as well as with each other, *coherent*—understandable, clear, evocative, and organized. At any moment, the meaning and organization of the visual and textual elements of the representation should be clear to participants (as well as practitioners) with "appropriateness of language, form, and structure to their purpose" as well as "completeness" and "persuasiveness" (Small, 2009: 266).

- In any facilitated session involving any sort of visual representation, whether a whiteboard, flipchart/easel sheet, or hypermedia software maps projected in front of a room, the value of the display is largely related to the degree to which the participants are *engaged* with it—looking at it, talking about it, referring to it, involved in its construction or reshaping.

- The representation should, as much as possible, be adding value for the participants and helping to fulfill the goals of the session, the participants, and the larger effort of which the session is a part. It is the responsibility of the practitioner to make sure that the representation is a useful part of the proceedings. *Usefulness* refers to the extent to which the representation appears to be adding value for the participants and helping to fulfill the predetermined or emergent goals of the session.

Each of the three CEU criteria could be further broken down into types or dimensions. For example, one could speak of any of the criteria in terms of visual, textual, hypertextual, interpersonal, etc. A criterion like "engagement" can be viewed on many levels: engagement with the map as viewers, engagement with the map as makers, engagement with facilitation, engagement with each other, and so on. The ratings are not value judgments on the quality of the session, but rather the degree to which the three dimensions are being fulfilled, especially with regard to a representation.

The tool is applied as follows. Recordings of a session, such as audio, video and screen recordings, are divided into timeslots. Each timeslot is assessed in terms of the CEU of the relationship of the participants to the representational display. There are three ratings: High (three points), indicating a high or strong degree of engagement, coherence, and usefulness; Medium (two points), indicating a medium or average degree of the three criteria; and Low (one point), indicating that there was a low degree during that timeslot. Table 6.3 provides a set of examples from participatory knowledge mapping sessions illustrating how each rating can be derived from observation of recorded data. Each individual rating is derived from the specifics of the session and timeslot itself, and thus they vary in the salient aspects that can be discerned from a recording. Ratings can be assigned based on participant comments, observations of practitioner actions, and by examining the representational artifact itself at that moment in time in the context of the current participant statements or actions.

Table 6.3: CEU ratings and examples

Criteria	Low	Medium	High
Coherence	The representation is unclear or bears little fidelity to the current focus of interest; e.g., a participant remarks that "I do not see what we're talking about" on the map	Moderate level of coherence, e.g., some confusion about the meaning of the way various items on the map are tagged, but generally the representation is clear enough to follow	The representation is a clear reflection of the discussion or exercise, in form, content and organization. All participant contributions have clear places to be entered and linked on the map
Engagement	The participants are paying little or no attention to the map, e.g., some participants are having a side conversation with no reference to the map	Participants start to make side conversation while practitioners are in the midst of making a complicated change to the map, rendering it temporarily less than clear	Participants are looking at, talking about, and appearing to care about what is on a map; e.g., a participant validates that the way the practitioner has captured his/her input on the map is accurate
Usefulness	The representation is not acting as a tool toward the realization of the session's purpose, e.g., the map is no longer keeping up with either the intended exercise or the emergent conversation	It is partially, but not completely, clear to the participants how the map will help them complete their current exercise	The representation is integral to the achievement of the session's purpose, e.g., the structure put in place for the exercise is working efficiently; participants understand the sequence of events and actions

For example, the representation in a specific timeslot might display a high degree of clarity and "readability"; all the content is legibly presented and laid out, and is faithful to the statements, tone, and purpose of the meeting (at least of its current activity). Thus, both Coherence and Usefulness would be rated as High (3 points each). However, at that moment the participants are caught up in a side discussion and are not paying attention to the representation, therefore Engagement would be rated as Low (1 point). Figure 6.3 shows the various components of a CEU analysis.

By assigning a color to each rating, *heat maps* are generated that provide a gestalt visualization of the whole session in terms of the three criteria. Figure 6.4 shows the comparison of CEU heat maps from eight studied sessions. Such heat maps make it possible to identify the overall tenor of each session, and to point out where sensemaking moments, or breakdowns, may have occurred—typically when the 3s (high ratings, green shading) drop to 2s (yellow) or 1s (red), indicating that the representational artifact seemed to add little or no value at that moment. When a session has high ratings throughout, it can indicate that the preparation and execution of the session (design and realization) were both well thought out in advance and handled in practice. In such sessions, possible breakdowns are avoided, often through the expertise of a practitioner.

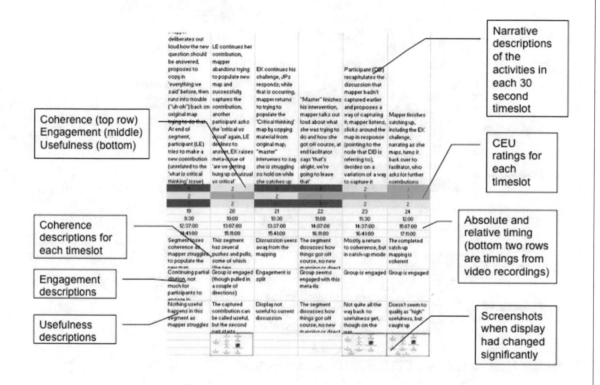

Figure 6.3: Components of a CEU analysis.

Figure 6.4 shows an overview of the sensemaking character from eight sessions that we studied. This visualization shows that three of the sessions (Ames Groups 1, 2, and 3) contain a fair amount of red cells, indicating low ratings for one or more of the CEU elements (possibly reflecting the relatively novice level of most of those sessions' practitioners, though there is no inherent correlation between low ratings and practitioner skill). These are moments in the sessions when things went somewhat awry, in terms of the practitioners' intentions for having the group co-construct the representation. These would be prime locations to look for sensemaking triggers (what set off the drop in the ratings), as well as what the practitioners or participants did to restore the session to better functioning. The remaining sessions had few or no drops, indicating that the practitioners and participants experienced relatively unproblematic going (it might also mean that practitioner interventions, or participant actions, helped save what might otherwise have been more problematic occurences, as we saw in the Hab Crew case study). Black rectangles indicate the segments selected for analysis as sensemaking episodes.

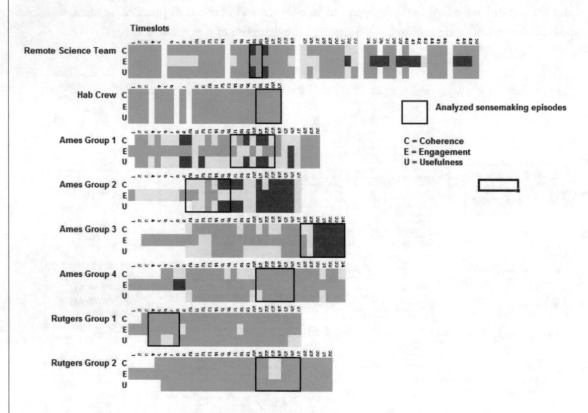

Figure 6.4: Heat maps from a CEU analysis of several sessions.

Within the methodology, after reviewing the Shaping form and CEU analysis for a session, a particular sensemaking episode may be selected for closer analysis, which starts with a narrative description of the episode.

6.3   SENSEMAKING EPISODE DESCRIPTION

These are narrative descriptions, which provide a rich delineation of a sensemaking episode within a session. For this, a starting and ending point for the episode is identified, from the point of the sensemaking trigger (an event or anomaly that initiates some sensemaking behavior) to its resolution or culmination. Sometimes there is no resolution per se, for example, when practitioners are not able to bring a session back on track after a breakdown. This can happen when participants cease engaging with the representation and just talk to each other without any reference to the representation (related to the Engagement element of CEU analysis). It's important to try to capture the nuances of the sensemaking trigger, practitioner and participant actions and responses, and any outcomes, to trace the character of sensemaking that occurred. Figure 6.5 shows a small portion of a Sensemaking Episode description for a team of scientists working through a planning exercise (see the Hab Crew case study in Chapter 4).

Figure 1: Session at 51:17

They proceed with this unproblematically, identifying additional names, until M voices some confusion with the naming approach in general:

> [52:15]
> M: "...I don't understand how you use these, but you do, right? It's letter letter? Is that what it is?" A: [52:19-20] "Yeah"
> A: "So our sample bag would be, like, S F slash um 2 1 slash zero 1. And that would be, um"

In the midst of this M. makes an (unprompted) grouping of the nomenclature nodes captured so far, using a Question node:

> M: "So this is letter letter right?"
> A: "Yeah that's all goes there in front of it"
> A: "And then ..."

Figure 6.5: Portion of a Sensemaking Episode description.

Writing out a narrative description in this manner focuses the analysis on the place each move or choice had in the way the sensemaking episode unfolded. The Moves and Choices analysis drills down into even a finer level of detail.

6.4   MOVES AND CHOICES ANALYSIS

The Moves and Choices analysis looks at each practitioner utterance, participant statement, or representational move for a sensemaking episode according to a number of criteria. This provides a fine-grained understanding of various dimensions of each move, such as the degree and kind of participant engagement with the representation at that moment; the engagement of the practitioner with the participants (e.g., acting in direct response to direction from a participant, or working off to the side to clean up some aspect of the map, or preparing for an upcoming event); the aspects of the setting on which practitioners were focused for that move (participants, maps, text, subject matter, surroundings, or process), and other factors. Mapping each move on the Moves and Choices grid requires careful consideration about what that move meant in the context of both the session as a whole and within the particular sensemaking episode, sensitizing the analysis in terms of the meaning to both participants and practitioners. Table 6.4 shows a portion of the taxonomy of concepts used in the Moves and Choices analysis.

Table 6.4: Move-by-move analysis schema for Moves and Choices analysis	
Aspect	**Description**
Participant Verbal Statements	Transcript of any participant utterance made in the course of a move
Practitioner Verbal Statements	Transcript of any practitioner utterance made in the course of a move
Move Type	Assigns each practitioner move to a type in a taxonomy of moves with the representational tools in use (e.g., Node Move-Arranging, Navigate-Map Open, etc.), or Verbal move types (Statement/Announcement, Acknowledgment, Query, Helpful Comment, Exclamation)
Participant Engagement with Representation	Characterizes the degree to which participants are paying attention to the representation during the move. Possible values: Active, Direct, Delinked, Partial, and Unclear. The Active value, which refers to moments when participants are directing the practitioner to perform particular actions on the representation, has the subtypes Text, Validation, Navigation, and Structure

Practitioner Response/ Engagement Mode	Characterizes the degree to which the practitioner is engaged with the participants during the move. Possible values: Direct, Semi-Direct, Indirect, Delinked. Delinked refers to moves when practitioner attention is focused completely on manipulation of the representation, not interacting or responding to the participants
Practitioner Focus	Characterizes what the participant is paying attention to or working with during the move. Can be (and often is) multiple. Values: Participants, Maps, Text, Subject Matter, Surroundings, Process

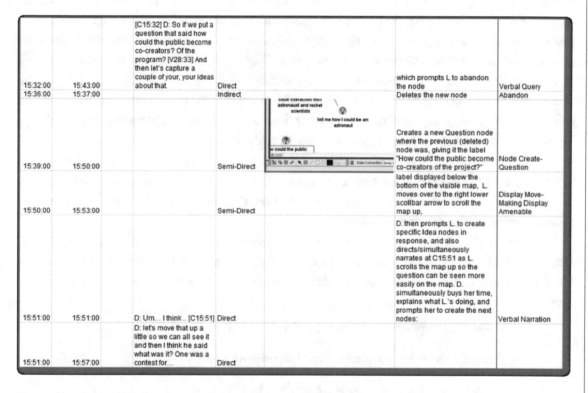

Figure 6.6: Portion of the Moves and Choices analysis from a session.

The example Moves and Choices analysis section shown in Figure 6.6 illustrates six practitioner moves: two verbal statements (at 14m 47s and 14m 51s) and four actions on the representation, at 14m 46s, 14m 48s, 14m 51s (at the same time as a verbal statement) and 14m 59s. Four of these moves were done with simultaneous focus on participants (engaged in conversation with them), maps (working on the form of the map), text (working with the text of the map's icons), and the subject matter of the session, while one (the Link move at 14:59) is a shaping move on the map itself.

The Moves and Choices analysis requires very close inspection and increased sensitivity to nuances of the data. The process demonstrates how much is going on when a skilled practitioner is at work, supporting a team with the artifacts and rationale it needs as their deliberations unfold. Moreover, the Moves and Choices analysis sets the stage for characterizing practitioner actions and choices according to a set of criteria derived from the experiential dimensions discussed in the previous chapter. This is called the Framing analysis.

6.5   FRAMING ANALYSIS

The Framing analysis characterizes practitioner actions during the session in aesthetic, ethical, and experiential terms. Reflecting the conceptual framework described in Chapter 3, the Framing analysis looks at how the practice and context interweave, and in what ways the aesthetic and ethical dimensions of the practice intertwine (McCarthy and Wright, 2004). It is a normative or ideal model against which to hold up situations of practice (Aakhus, 2007; Aakhus and Jackson, 2004). Kolbe and Boos (2009) advocate using a normative model to study facilitator subjectivity. Such a model can be used as a diagnostic tool to analyze what factors are preventing a situation from achieving its potential, or at least to characterize a practice situation in potentially useful ways.

The model used in the Framing analysis provides a set of components, elements, and exploratory questions to help determine how a context of service, the unique set of people, and the goals, constraints, situation, and subject matter can inform the shaping the practitioner performs on the representational object(s), and vice versa.

The model contains three major categories or components of the practitioner's stance—his/her orientation toward various aspects of the situation or practice setting: the practitioner's towards him/herself and his/her own actions, towards the participants, and towards the situation as a whole. These are:

(A) toward the practitioner's own involvement (self in situation);

(B) toward the other people involved (participants); and

(C) toward the event or experience as a whole.

The **Element** column in Table 6.5 breaks down each stance into elements, each of which is related to the body of theory from which it arises. These elements constitute an ideal model of practitioner stance; that is, the model specifies the preferred conduct of a practitioner as *maintaining a dialogic orientation, fostering a heightened degree of connection between participants, the setting, purpose, and representation*, and so on. The elements in turn generate descriptive (characterizing) or normative (evaluating) questions that can help guide the analysis of a particular setting, found in the **Descriptive and Normative Questions** column.

Considering the questions put forward in the Framing model involves examining and reflecting on the analytical artifacts produced thus far. Since the Framing analysis comes last in the methodology, by this time an analyst will be very familiar with the specific occurrences in a session, and particularly with the nuances of the behavior demonstrated by the practitioners during sensemaking episodes.

For example, the Framing analysis of the Ames Group 2 session had the following responses for component *A.5 (mediated objects and other interventions should preserve openness and dialogicity)*:

> *How do the actions of the practitioners inhibit openness and dialogicity?*

> The prepared map appeared (and was said by participants afterward to be) too complex and involved for participants to engage with, although the mapping of the "needs" section did seem to invite dialogue (unfortunately shut off by the mapper). The mapper's verbal intervention served to inhibit the nascent discussion about how to map the "needs" section.

In this case, a diagnosis for improving practice is that the practitioners needed either to be flexible in how the session would proceed and evolve the map accordingly (with its extensive pre-structuring that the participants were not paying attention to), or needed to intervene again to bring the session back to the course that they had intended. They could have brought the attention of the group to the portion of the map that contained the desired area of focus and created an effective way for the group to engage with it. As it happened, they stood by and waited to see if the conversation would come back to the intended course of its own accord (rarely an effective strategy).

Table 6.5: Framing analysis components

Element	Descriptive and Normative Questions
Component A: Towards the practitioner's own involvement (self in situation)	
(A.1) Imposing their own coherence and values on a situation	• What coherence is the practitioner imposing on the situation? • What values is the practitioner imposing on the situation? • In what ways are these congruent (or not) with those of the participants

(A.2) Constructing narratives to account for how the situation arrived at the current pass/breaches in canonicity	• What is the narrative the practitioner is using to construct the situation? • What is its degree of internal consistency? • How evocative and inclusive is it? • How useful is it?
(A.3) Eliminating prejudices and preconceptions	• What prejudices may be active? • What preconceptions may be active? • What personal desires or goals may be active?
(A.4) Personal authenticity in the practice setting	• In what ways is the practitioner acting in an authentic manner (vs. received, affected, etc.)?
(A.5) Mediated objects and other interventions should preserve openness and dialogicity	• How do the representations the practitioner constructs or modifies foster openness and dialogicity? • How do they inhibit them?
(A.6) Artifacts should be clear, expressive, and helpful	• How clear are the artifacts produced/modified by the practitioner? • How expressive are they? • How helpful are they within the context of practice?
(A.7) Perseverance in the face of checks and resistance	• What checks to forward progress does the practitioner encounter? • What resistance from participants, materials, etc. occurs? • How does the practitioner respond in the face of these?
(A.8) Clear and focused communication	• How clear is the practitioner's verbal communication? • In what ways does the practitioner maintain focus on the aspects of importance in the situation?
Element	**Descriptive and Normative Questions**
Component B: Towards the other people involved (participants, stakeholders, and others)	
(B.1) The importance of participants' impulses and desires; attention to what may be bothering or affecting participants	• What observable or discoverable participant impulses, desires, or other factors are operating in the situation? • How does the practitioner address these?

Element	Descriptive and Normative Questions
(B.2) Unfinalizability; preserve room for surprise, imagination, and creativity to emerge	• In what ways do the practitioner's actions reflect an attitude of unfinalizability toward the participants and their interests, concerns, and agency? • In what ways does the practitioner preserve or close off room for surprise, imagination, and creativity to emerge?
(B.3) Dialogic orientation	• How do the practitioner's actions and communication open up or close off dialogue in the situation? • In what ways does the practitioner display openness and sensitivity to the different participant voices (vs. summarizing them into abstractions or types)?
Element	**Descriptive and Normative Questions**
Component C: Towards the event or experience as a whole	
(C.1) Heightened degree of connection between people, setting, purpose, and medium	• How do the practitioner's actions help create this kind of connection and integration? • In what ways are the distinctions or boundaries between people, setting, objects, etc. made stronger or lesser?
(C.2) High level and quality of communication	• How does the practitioner elevate (or diminish) the level and quality of communication in the practice setting?
(C.3) Importance of the past as the background and context to the practice setting	• In what ways does the practitioner reference or bring in elements of past work, ideas, or events? • Are such "background" elements combined with "foreground" (current) concerns, ideas, or representations?
(C.4) The relationships of parts to parts and to the whole	• How does the practitioner focus on both individual details and the relationships of those details to the "big picture" and each other? • How are the moves from parts to whole accomplished?

6.6   GRANULARITY OF THE DIFFERENT TECHNIQUES

Figure 6.7 shows the relative granularity of these analysis techniques. The Shaping and Framing analysis looks at the whole-session level, seeking to describe overall shaping behavior and framing considerations characterizing practitioner actions during a session. The CEU analysis aims both to give a concise picture of the trajectory of a session as a whole, from start to finish, but also to characterize the coherence, engagement, and usefulness of timeslots within a session. The Sensemaking Episode description and Moves and Choices analyses provide finer-grained looks at specific choices and moves in the context of one or more timeslots, focusing on sensemaking moments where anomalies or other triggers cause sensemaking behavior on the part of practitioners. In the course of the individual session analyses, insights from each of the analysis techniques employed help ensure completeness and accuracy of the others, often prompting revisions in earlier analysis documents as new insights emerge.

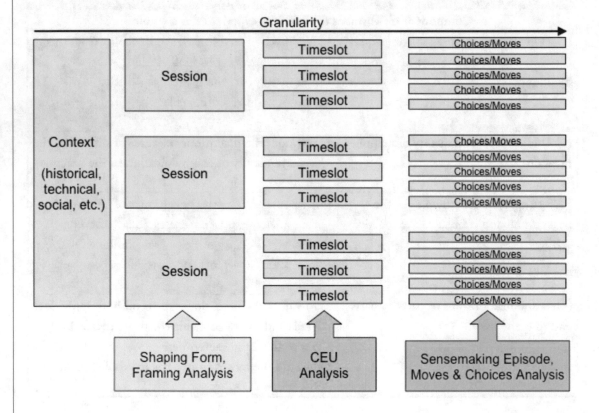

Figure 6.7: Granularity of analysis techniques.

6.7   HOW THE TECHNIQUES RELATE TO THE CONCEPTUAL FRAMEWORK

Taken together, these analysis techniques form an integrated method that can be applied to diverse instances of practice. Figure 6.8 shows how the tools map onto the conceptual dimensions described in Chapter 3. As the small x's indicate, each of the tools helps reveal each of the experiential dimensions via analysis of practice. The large bold X's indicate the special emphasis of a tool in theoretical terms. The Sensemaking Episode descriptions as well as CEU analyses give particular focus to events in a session that require a practitioner to engage in sensemaking behavior, and the ensuing improvised actions they take. The Shaping Form and Framing analyses encourage attention to the aesthetic dimensions of practitioner actions in a session, placing them in an overall narrative context and highlighting the ethical meaning and consequences of those actions in that context. Comparative analysis of data gathered through applying all of these tools provides a nuanced portrayal of the experiential dimensions of representational practice.

	Sensemaking Episode	Moves and Choices	Shaping Form	CEU Analysis	Framing Analysis
Aesthetics	x	x	X	x	X
Narrative	x	x	X	x	X
Improvisation	X	x	x	X	x
Sensemaking	X	x	x	X	x
Ethics	x	x	X	x	X

Figure 6.8: Relating the conceptual dimensions to the analysis tools.

6.8   SUMMARY

This Appendix described five different analytical lenses that reveal the experiential dimensions of participatory representational practice discussed in Chapter 3. The analysis approach focuses on characterizing how choices made by practitioners in their preparation period are enacted during their sessions. Moments where practitioners were faced with some kind of anomaly in the course of a session are selected for closer analysis, looking at the specific practitioner moves and choices that determined the outcome of the sensemaking moment, focusing on the aesthetic, ethical, improvisational, and narrative aspects of those moves and how these contribute to the ways in which participants engage with the representation, with special emphasis on the character of the real-time shaping of the representation.

Shedding light on facilitative practitioner actions, sensemaking, and effectiveness, requires understanding all three in context. We put special emphasis on the ways that facilitative visual representations become coherent (clear, expressive, evocative, informative), engaging (compelling enough to pay attention to and involve in a session's communicative discourse) and useful (applicable to and supportive of the reason participants are working together, their end product and goal).

Using such tools allows the discovery of insights deriving both from "grounded," bottom-up data, themes and categories that emerge from observations, and "top-down" analysis starting from the Framing model and conceptual framework. They enable data to be examined at both "whole session" levels, comparing summative characteristics of sessions with each other, and at the level of specific events, moves, and practitioner choices within sessions, often those performed by an individual such as a mapper or a facilitator.

Bibliography

Aakhus, M. (2001). Technocratic and Design Stances toward Communication Expertise: How GDSS Facilitators Understand their Work. *Journal of applied communication research*, Volume 29, Number 4, November 2001. DOI: 10.1080/00909880128113.

Aakhus, M. (2003). Neither Naïve Nor Critical Reconstruction: Dispute Mediators, Impasse, and the Design of Argumentation. *Argumentation* 17: 265-290. DOI: 10.1023/A:1025112227381.

Aakhus, M. (2004). Understanding the Socio-Technical Gap: A Case of GDSS Facilitation. In G. Goldkuhl, M. Lind, and S. Cronholm (Eds.), *Proceedings of the 2d International Conference on Action in Language, Organizations, and Information Systems* (pp. 137-148). Linkšping, Sweden: Research Network VITS.

Aakhus, M. (2007). Conversations for Reflection: Augmenting Transitions and Transformations in Expertise. In: McInerney, C., Day, R. (Eds.), *Rethinking Knowledge Management: Information Science and Knowledge Management*. DOI: 10.1007/3-540-71011-6_1.

Aakhus, M., Jackson, S. (2004). Technology, Interaction, and Design. In K. Fitch and R. Sanders (Eds.), *Handbook of Language and SocialInteraction*. Mahwah, NJ: Lawrence Erlbaum. DOI: 10.1111/j.1540-4781.2007.00639_4.x.

Alexander, B. (2010). *Is William Martinez Not Our Brother?: Twenty Years of the Prison Creative Arts Project*. Ann Arbor: University of Michigan Press. DOI: 10.3998/nps.8582521.0001.001.

Arnheim, R. (1967). *Art and Visual Perception: A Psychology of the Creative Eye*. Berkeley And Los Angeles: University of California Press.

ATC21S (2012). 21st Century Skills. University of Sydney/Cisco/Intel/Microsoft: Assessment and Teaching of 21st Century Skills. http://atc21s.org/wp-content/uploads/2011/11/1-Defining-21st-Century-Skills.pdf.

Bailey, J. (2008). First Steps in Qualitative Data Analysis: Transcribing. *Family Practice* Volume 25, Issue 2 Pp. 127-131. DOI: 10.1093/fampra/cmn003.

Bardzell, S. (2010). Feminist HCI: Taking Stock and Outlining an Agenda for Design. *Proceedings of CHI 2010*. DOI: 10.1145/1753326.1753521.

Benjamin, R. (2001). Mediation as Theater and Negotiation as Performance Art. First published in the ACR (Association for Conflict Resolution) Family Section Newsletter, Fall, 2001. Found online at http://www.mediate.com//articles/benjamin5.cfm (13 Feb 2011).

Bergvall-Kåreborn, B., Ståhlbrost, A. (2008). Participatory Design—One Step Back or Two Steps Forward? *Proceedings of the Tenth Anniversary Conference on Participatory Design 2008*, Bloomington, Indiana October 01 - 04, 2008. New York: ACM Press.

Bertelsen, O., Pold, S. (2004). Criticism as an Approach to Interface Aesthetics. *NordiCHI '04*, October 23-27, 2004 Tampere, Finland. pp. 23-32. DOI: 10.1145/1028014.1028018.

Bishop, S., Helbing, D. (2012) (Eds.) Special Issue: Participatory Science and Computing for Our Complex World. *European Physical Journal Special Topics* 214: 1-666. DOI: 10.1140/epjst/e2012-01684-1.

Blomberg, J., Henderson, A. (1990). Reflections on Participatory Design: Lessons from the Trillium Experience. *Proceedings of ACM CHI '90 Conference on Human Factors in Computing Systems*, pp. 353-359. New York: ACM Press. DOI: 10.1145/97243.97307.

Bødker, S., Iversen, O. (2002). Staging a Professional Participatory Design Practice: Moving PD beyond the Initial Fascination of User Involvement. *NordiCHI '02* pp. 11-18. DOI: 10.1145/572020.572023.

Boehner, K., Sengers, P., Warner, S. (2008). Interfaces with the Ineffable: Meeting Aesthetic Experience on its Own Terms. *ACM Transactions on Computer-Human Interaction*, v. 15, 3, Article 12 (November 2008). DOI: 10.1145/1453152.1453155.

Bostrom, R., Anson, R., Clawson, V. (1993). Group Facilitation and Group Support Systems. *Group Support Systems: New Perspectives*, Macmillan, 146-148.

Bratteteig, T., Wagner, I. (2014). Analyzing the Politics of PD: A Conceptual Investigation. *PDC 2014 Call For Participation*, accessed online at http://www.pdcpolitics.no/ Aug 18 2014.

Bruner, J. (1990). *Acts of Meaning*. Cambridge: Harvard University Press.

Buckingham Shum, S. (2007). Hypermedia Discourse: Contesting Networks of Ideas and Arguments. Keynote Address, *Proc. 15th International Conference on Conceptual Structures*, Sheffield, July 2007. Lecture Notes in Computer Science, Volume 4604/2007, pp.29-44. Berlin: Springer. DOI: 10.1007/978-3-540-73681-3_3.

Buckingham Shum, S. (2012). Learning Analytics. Policy Briefing, UNESCO Institute for Information Technologies in Education. http://www.iite.unesco.org/publications/3214711.

Buckingham Shum, S., Aberer, K., Schmidt, A., Bishop, S., Lukowicz, P., Anderson, S., Charalabidis, Y., Domingue, D., de Freitas, S., Dunwell, I., Edmonds, B., Grey, F., Haklay, M., Jelasity, M., Karpištšenko, A., Kohlhammer, J., Lewis, J., Pitt, J., Sumner, R., Helbing, D. (2012). Towards a Global Participatory Platform: Democratising Open Data, Complexity Science and Collective Intelligence. *European Physical Journal Special Topics*, 214(1) pp. 109–152. http://link.springer.com/article/10.1140/epjst/e2012-01690-3.

Buckingham Shum, S., Deakin Crick, R. (2012). Learning Dispositions and Transferable Compe-
tencies: Pedagogy, Modelling and Learning Analytics. *Proceedings of the 2nd International
Conference on Learning Analytics and Knowledge.* Vancouver, 29 Apr-2 May: ACM: New
York, 92-101. DOI: 10.1145/2330601.2330629 Eprint: http://oro.open.ac.uk/32823.

Bush, R., Folger, J. (1994). *The Promise of Mediation: The Transformative Approach to Conflict.* Jossey-
Bass Publishers, San Francisco.

Cashtan, M. (2005). The Gift of Self: The Art of Transparent Facilitation. *The IAF Handbook of
Group Facilitation: Best Practices from the Leading Organization in Facilitation.* Pp. 573-
590. Edited By Sandy Schuman, San Francisco: Jossey-Bass. Accessed online 7/18/10:
http://books.google.com/books?id=JWefPo9uEhQC&printsec=frontcover.

Chadwick, R. (1998). Professional Ethics. In E. Craig (Ed.), *Routledge Encyclopedia of Philosophy.*
London: Routledge. Retrieved February 26, 2011, from http://www.rep.routledge.com/
article/L077.

Chin, G., Rosson, M. (1998). Progressive Design: Staged Evolution of Scenarios in the Design
of a Collaborative Science Learning Environment. *Proceedings CHI 98: Human Factors in Computing Systems,* (Los Angeles, CA), 611-618. New York: ACM Press. DOI:
10.1145/274644.274726.

Clancey, W., Sierhuis, M., Alena, R., Berrios, D., Dowding, J., Graham, J., Tyree, K., Hirsh, R.,
Garry, W., Semple, A., Buckingham Shum, S., Shadbolt, N., Rupert, S. (2005). Automat-
ing CapCom Using Mobile Agents and Robotic Assistants. In *Proceedings of the American
Institute of Aeronautics and Astronautics 1st space exploration conference,* 31 Jan–1 Feb, 2005.

Clark, B. (2008). Resources for Action in the Negotiation of Participatory Design Projects. *Proceedings Participatory Design Conference 2008.* New York: CPSR/ACM.

Claxton, G. (1999). *Wise Up: The Challenge of Lifelong Learning,* London: Bloomsbury.

Cohen, C. (1997). *A Poetics of Reconciliation: The Aesthetic Mediation of Conflict.* Unpublished Ph.D.
dissertation, University of New Hampshire, December 1997. Available online at www.
brandeis.edu/ethics/coexistence_initiative/research_and_scholarship/reconciliation.pdf.

Conklin, J. (2005). *Dialogue Mapping: Building Shared Understanding of Wicked Problems.* Chiches-
ter: Wiley.

Cooks, L., Hale, C. (1994). The Construction of Ethics in Mediation. *Conflict resolution quarterly,*
Volume 12, Issue 1, pages 55–76, Autumn (Fall) 1994.

Deakin Crick. R. (2006). *Learning Power in Practice: A Guide for Teachers,* London: Paul Chapman.
DOI: 10.4135/9780857025548.

Deakin Crick, R. (2007). Learning How to Learn: The Dynamic Assessment of Learning Power. *The Curriculum Journal* 18: 135-153. DOI: 10.1080/09585170701445947.

Deakin Crick, R. (2012). Student Engagement: Identity, Learning Power and Enquiry - A Complex Systems Approach. In: Christenson S, Reschly A and Wylie C (eds) *The Handbook of Research on Student Engagement* New York: Springer. DOI: 10.1007/978-1-4614-2018-7_32.

Deakin Crick, R., Stringher, C., and Ren, K (Eds.) (2014). *Learning to Learn: International Perspectives from Theory and Practice*. Routledge: London.

Dearden, A., Rizvi, H. (2008). Participatory IT Design and Participatory Development: A Comparative Review. *PDC '08: Proceedings of the Tenth Anniversary Conference on Participatory Design 2008*. New York: ACM. DOI: 10.1145/1795234.1795246.

Dervin, B. (1983). An Overview of Sense-Making Research: Concepts, Methods, and Results to date. Paper presented at the annual meeting of the International Communication Association, Dallas, TX.

Dervin, B. (1992). From the Mind's Eye of the User: The Sense-Making Qualitative-Quantitative Methodology. In Glazier, J., Powell, R., (eds.) *Qualitative research in information management*. Englewood, CO: Libraries Unlimited. pp. 61-84.

Dervin, B. (1997). Observing, Being Victimized by, and Colluding with isms (Sexism, Racism, Able-Bodyism): Sense-Making Interviews from a University Advanced Level Class in Interviewing. [On-line] Available: http://communication.sbs.ohio-state.edu/sense-making/inst/idervin97isms.html/.

Dervin, B. (1998). Sense-Making Theory and Practice: An Overview of User Interests in Knowledge Seeking and Use. In: *Journal of knowledge management*, Volume 2 Number 2. DOI: 10.1108/13673279810249369.

Dervin, B., Naumer, C. (2009). Sense-Making. *Encyclopedia of Communication Theory*, Edited by Stephen W. Littlejohn and Karen A. Foss. Los Angeles: Sage. Pp. 876-880. DOI: 10.4135/9781412959384.

Dewey, J. (1934). *Art as Experience*. New York: The Berkeley Publishing Group. Reprinted 2005.

DiSalvo, C., Boehner, K., Knouf, N., Sengers, P. (2009). Nourishing the Ground for Sustainable HCI: Considerations from Ecologically Engaged Art. *CHI 2009*, April 4-9, 2009, Boston, Massachusetts, USA. DOI: 10.1145/1518701.1518763.

Dissanayake, E. (1988). *What is Art For?* Seattle: University of Washington Press.

Dowmunt, T. (2003). Mother Pictures: An Autobiographical Video Work in Progress. *PARIP 2003*. Available online at http://www.bris.ac.uk/parip/webpaper_dowmunt.pdf.

Dreir, O. (1993). Re-Searching Psychotherapeutic Practice. In S. Chaiklin and J. Lave, Eds. *Understanding Practice: Perspectives on Activity and Context*. Cambridge: Cambridge University Press. DOI: 10.1017/CBO9780511625510.005.

Dweck, C. (1999). *Self Theories: Their Role in Motivation, Personality and Development*. Psychology Press: Philadelphia, PA.

Edmonds, E., Muller, L., Connell, M. (2006). On Creative Engagement. *Visual Communication*, 5; 307. DOI: 10.1177/1470357206068461.

Ellis, J. (2003). Research and the Problem of 'the Industry.' *Proceedings of PARIP 2003*. Available online at http://www.bris.ac.uk/parip/ellis.htm.

European Commission (2006). *The European Framework for Key Competences*. http://ec.europa.eu/education/lifelong-learning-policy/key_en.htm.

Fortner, R., Christians, C. (1981). Separating Wheat from Chaff in Qualitative Studies, in Stempel, G. and Westley, B., Eds., *Research Methods in Mass Communication*. 2nd ed. Englewood Cliffs: Prentice Hall.

Friedman, B. (1996). Value-Sensitive Design. *Interactions*, Volume 3 Issue 6, Nov./Dec. 1996, pages 16-23. DOI: 10.1145/242485.242493.

Frost, A., Yarrow, R. (1990). *Improvisation in Drama*. Hampshire: MacMillan Press.

Furnham, D. (2003). The Cinema of Comic Illusions. *Proceedings of PARIP 2003*. Available online at http://www.bris.ac.uk/parip/furnham.htm.

Goffman, E. (1967). *Interaction Ritual*. New York: Pantheon.

Greenbaum, J., Kyng, M. (1991). *Design at Work: Cooperative Design of Computer Systems*. (New York: Erlbaum). DOI: 10.1080/01449299208924335.

Hansen, H., Barry, D., Boje, D., Hatch, M. (2007). Truth or Consequences: An Improvised Collective Story Construction. *Journal of Management Inquiry*, June 2007 vol. 16 no. 2 112-126. DOI: 10.1177/1056492607302652.

Hartmann, J., Sutcliffe, A., De Angeli, A. (2008). Towards a Theory of User Judgment of Aesthetics and User Interface Quality. *ACM Trans. Comput.-Hum. Interact* 15, no. 4: 1-30. DOI: 10.1145/1460355.1460357.

Hecht, K., Maass, S. (2008). Teaching Participatory Design. In *Proceedings of 2008 Participatory Design Conference*. New York: ACM Press. DOI: 10.1145/1795234.1795262.

Helbing, D. (2013). Globally Networked Risks and How to Respond. *Nature* 497: 51-59. DOI: 10.1038/nature12047.

Hilberry, J. (2012). Outlaw Girl: The Challenge of Designing Poetry Exercises for an Organizational Context. *Organizational Aesthetics* Vol. 1: Iss. 1, 68-80. Available at: http://digitalcommons.wpi.edu/oa/vol1/iss1/6.

Iversen, O., Dindler, C. (2008). Pursuing Aesthetic Inquiry in Participatory Design. *Proceedings of PDC '2008*. pp.138~145. DOI: 10.1145/1795234.1795254.

Jacobs, S. (2002). Maintaining Neutrality in Dispute Mediation: Managing Disagreement while Managing Not to Disagree. *Journal of Pragmatics* 34. DOI: 10.1016/S0378-2166(02)00071-1.

Jacobs, S., Aakhus, M. (2002). How to Resolve a Conflict: Two Models of Dispute Resolution. In F. H. van Eemeren (Ed.), *Advances in Pragma-Dialectics* (pp. 29-44). Amsterdam: SICSAT.

Johansson, C., Heide, M. (2008). Speaking of Change: Three Communication Approaches in Studies of Organizational Change. *Corporate Communications: An International Journal*. Vol. 13 No. 3, pp. 288-305. DOI: 10.1108/13563280810893661.

Klein, G., Moon, B., Hoffman, R. (2006). Making Sense of Sensemaking 1: Alternative Perspectives. *IEEE Intelligent Systems* 21 (4, July/August), 70-73. DOI: 10.1109/MIS.2006.75.

Kolb, J., Jin, S., Hoon Song, J. (2008). A Model of Small Group Facilitator Competencies. *Performance Improvement Quarterly*, 21: 119-133. DOI: 10.1002/piq.20026.

Kolbe, M., Boos, M. (2009). Facilitating Group Decision-Making: Facilitator's Subjective Theories on Group Coordination. *Forum Qualitative Sozialforschung / Forum: Qualitative Social Research*, 10(1), Art. 28, http://nbn-resolving.de/urn:nbn:de:0114-fqs0901287. *Qualitative Research on Intercultural Communication*, Vol 10, No 1. Edited by Matthias Otten, Jens Allwood, Maria Assumpta Aneas, Dominic Busch, David Hoffman and Michele Schweisfurth. Available online at http://www.qualitative-research.net/index.php/fqs/article/viewArticle/1244/2692.

Kurtz, C., Snowden, D. (2003). The New Dynamics of Strategy: Sense-Making in a Complex and Complicated World. *IBM Systems Journal*, Vol 42, No 3. DOI: 10.1147/sj.423.0462.

Lai, E., Viering, M. (2012). Assessing 21st Century Skills: Integrating Research Findings. National Council on Measurement in Education, Vancouver BC and Pearson Center for Digital Data, Analytics and Adaptive Learning. http://researchnetwork.pearson.com/wp-content/uploads/Assessing_21st_Century_Skills_NCME.pdf.

Levina, N. (2001). *Multi-Party Information Systems Development: The Challenge of Cross-Boundary Collaboration*. Unpublished PhD dissertation, Massachusetts Institute of Technology.

Lovelace, A. (2001). Story in Art and Mediation. In *Motion Magazine*, October 7, 2001. Available online at http://www.inmotionmagazine.com/al/alths1.html.

Lundberg, J., Arvola, M. (2007). Lessons Learned from Facilitation in Collaborative Design. *Eighth Australasian User Interface Conference*, Ballarat, Australia. Conferences in Research and Practice in Information Technology, Vol. 64. pp 51-54.

Macfarlane, J. (2002). Mediating Ethically: The Limits of Codes of Conduct and the Potential of a Reflective Practice Model. *Osgoode Hall Law Journal*, 49.

McCarthy, J., Wright, P. (2004). *Technology as Experience*. Cambridge, MA: MIT Press. DOI: 10.1145/1015530.1015549.

Merkel, C., Xiao, L., Farooq, U., Ganoe, C., Lee, R., Carroll, J., Rosson, M. (2004). Participatory Design in Community Computing Contexts: Tales from the Field. *Proceedings Participatory Design Conference 2004*. Toronto, Canada. New York: ACM. DOI: 10.1145/1011870.1011872.

Miller, J., Friedman, B., Jancke, G. (2007). Value Tensions in Design: The Value Sensitive Design, Development, and Appropriation of a Corporation's Groupware System. *GROUP '07: Proceedings of the 2007 International ACM Conference on Supporting Group Work*. ACM, New York. DOI: 10.1145/1316624.1316668.

Muhren, W., Van Den Eede, G., Van de Walle, B. (2008). Sensemaking and Implications for Information Systems Design: Findings from the Democratic Republic of Congo's Ongoing Crisis. *Information technology for development*. Volume 14, Issue 3. DOI: 10.1002/itdj.20104.

Muller, M. (1991). PICTIVE—An Exploration in Participatory Design. *Proceedings of ACM CHI '91 Conference on Human Factors in Computing Systems*, New Orleans, USA, 225-231. New York: ACM Press. DOI: 10.1145/108844.108896.

Murray, K. (1995). Narrative Partitioning: The Ins and Outs of Identity Construction. J. Smith, R. Harré, and Luk van Langenhove (eds). *Rethinking Psychology: Volume 1 - Conceptual Foundations*. London: Sage. Available online at http://home.mira.net/~kmurray/psych/in&out.html.

Nachmanovitch, S. (1990). *Free Play: Improvisation in Life and Art*. New York: Jeremy P. Tarcher/Putnam.

National Research Council (2011). Assessing 21st Century Skills: Summary of a Workshop. J.A. Koenig, Rapporteur. Committee on the Assessment of 21st Century Skills. Board on Testing and Assessment, Division of Behavioral and Social Sciences and Education.

OECD (2001). *Defining and Selecting Key Competencies*, Paris: OECD.

Okada, A., Buckingham Shum, S., Sherborne, T. (Eds.), (2008). *Knowledge Cartography: Software Tools and Mapping Techniques*. London: Springer. DOI: 10.1007/978-1-84800-149-7_7.

Osthoff, S. (1997). Lygia Clark and Hélio Oiticica: A Legacy of Interactivity and Participation for a Telematic Future. Leonardo On-Line, MIT Press. *Leonardo* Volume 30, No. 4 (1997). Available online at http://mitpress2.mit.edu/e-journals/Leonardo/isast/spec.projects/osthoff/osthoff.html.

Payne, M. (2006). *Narrative Therapy: An Introduction for Counselors*. London: Sage. DOI: 10.4135/9781446213322.

Rittel, H., Webber, M. (1973). Dilemmas in a General Theory of Planning. *Policy Sciences* 4: 155-169. DOI: 10.1007/BF01405730.

Russell, D., Stefik, M., Pirolli, P., Card, S. (1993). The Cost Structure of Sensemaking. *Proceedings of Inter CHI '93*, pp. 269-276. DOI: 10.1145/169059.169209.

Salverson, J. (2001). *Performing Testimony: Ehics, Pedagogy, and a Theatre beyond Injury*. Unpublished Ph.D. dissertation, University of Toronto.

Sawyer, K. (1996). The Semiotics of Improvisation: The Pragmatics of Musical and Verbal Performance. *Semiotica*, 108 (3/4). DOI: 10.1515/semi.1996.108.3-4.269.

Sawyer, K. (1997). Improvisational Theater: An Ethnotheory of Conversational Practice. *Creativity in Performance*, pp. 171-193, 1997.

Sawyer, K. (1999). Improvised Conversations: Music, Collaboration, and Development. *Psychology of Music*, 27, 2, 192-205. DOI: 10.1177/0305735699272009.

Sawyer, K. (2001). The Improvisational Performance of Everyday Life. *Journal of Mundane Behavior*, 2(2). On-line journal available at www.mundanebehavior.org.

Sawyer, K. (2003). *Group Creativity: Music, Theater, Collaboration*. Mahwah NJ: Lawrence Erlbaum. DOI: 10.1177/0305735606061850.

Sawyer, K. (2004). Creative Teaching: Collaborative Discourse as Disciplined Improvisation. *Educational researcher*, Vol. 33, No. 2, pp. 12–20. DOI: 10.3102/0013189X033002012.

Schön, D. (1983). *The Reflective Practitioner: How Professionals Think in Action*. London: Basic Books.

Schön, D. (1987). *Educating the Reflective Practitioner: Toward a New Design for Teaching and Learning in the Professions*. San Francisco: Jossey-Bass.

Selvin, A. M. (2011). *Making Representations Matter: Understanding Practitioner Experience in Participatory Sensemaking*. Doctoral Dissertation, Knowledge Media Institute, The Open University, UK. Available online at http://oro.open.ac.uk/30834.

Selvin, A., Buckingham Shum, S. (2008). Narrative, Sensemaking, and Improvisation in Participatory Hypermedia Construction. Paper presented at the Sensemaking Workshop, *CHI*

2008: ACM Conference on Computer–Human Interaction, Florence, Italy. Available online at http://oro.open.ac.uk/19039.

Selvin, A., Buckingham Shum, S. (2009). Coherence, Engagement, and Usefulness as Sensemaking Criteria in Participatory Media Practice. Paper presented at the Sensemaking Workshop, *ACM Computer–Human Interaction (CHI) Conference*, Boston, MA, USA. Available online at http://oro.open.ac.uk/12910.

Shariq, S. (1998). Sense Making and Artifacts: An Exploration into the Role of Tools in Knowledge Management. *Journal of Knowledge Management*, Volume 2 Number 2, December 1998. DOI: 10.1108/13673279810249341.

Sierhuis, M., Buckingham Shum, S. (2008). Human–Agent Knowledge Cartography for e-Science: NASA Field Trials at the Mars Desert Research Station. In A. Okada, S. Buckingham Shum, and T. Sherborne (Eds.), *Knowledge Cartography: Software Tools and Mapping Techniques* (pp. 287–305). London: Springer-Verlag. DOI: 10.1007/978-1-84800-149-7_14.

Small, T. (2009). Assessing Enquiry-Based Learning: Developing Objective Criteria from Personal Knowledge. *Curriculum Journal*, Volume 20, Issue 3, pp. 253-270. DOI: 10.1080/09585170903195878.

Stewart, J. (2006). High-Performing (and Threshold) Competencies for Group Facilitators. *Journal of Change Management*, Dec. 2006, Vol. 6 Issue 4, p417-439. DOI: 10.1080/14697010601087115.

Strauss, A., Corbin, J. (1990). *Basics of Qualitative Research: Grounded Theory Procedures and Techniques*. Sage, Newbury Park, 1990. DOI: 10.4135/9781452230153.

Suchman, L. (2003). *Located Accountabilities in Technology Production*. Published by the Centre for Science Studies, Lancaster University, Lancaster LA1 4YN, UK. Available online at http://www.comp.lancs.ac.uk/sociology/papers/Suchman-Located-Accountabilities.pdf.

Thomas, G. (2008). The Theories and Practices of Facilitator Educators: Conclusions from a Naturalistic Inquiry. *Group facilitation: a research and applications journal*, Number 9, 2008. DOI: 10.7459/ept/30.2.02.

Tracy, K. (1989). Conversational Dilemmas and the Naturalistic Experiment. In B. Dervin, L. Grossberg, B. O'Keefe, and E. Wartella (Eds.), *Rethinking Communication: Volume 2 Paradigm Examples* (pp. 411-423). Newbury Park, CA: Sage.

Tyler, C., Valek, L., Rowland, R. (2005). Graphic Facilitation and Large-Scale Interventions: Supporting Dialogue between Cultures at a Global, Multicultural, Interfaith

Event. *Journal of Applied Behavioral Science*, March 2005 vol. 41 no. 1 139-152. DOI: 10.1177/0021886304272850.

Udsen, L., Jørgensen, A. (2005). The Aesthetic Turn: Unravelling Recent Aesthetic Approaches to Human-Computer Interaction. *Digital creativity* 2005. Vol. 16. No. 4, pp. 205-216. DOI: 10.1080/14626260500476564.

van Vuuren, M., Elving, W. (2008). Communication, Sensemaking and Change as a Chord of Three Strands. *Corporate Communications: An International Journal*. Vol. 13 No. 3, pp. 349-359. DOI: 10.1108/1356328081093706.

Wagner, E., Piccoli, G. (2007). Moving beyond User Participation to Achieve Successful IS Design. *Commun. ACM* 50(12); pp.51-55. DOI: 10.1145/1323688.1323694.

Weick, K. (1995). *Sensemaking in Organizations*. Thousand Oaks, CA: Sage.

Weick, K., Sutcliffe, K., Obstfeld, D. (2005). Organizing and the Process of Sensemaking. *Organization Science*, 16(4): 409-421. DOI: 10.1287/orsc.1050.0133.

Weick, K., Meader, D. (1993). Sensemaking and Group Support Systems, in L. Jessup and J. Valacich, eds., *Group Support Systems: New Perspectives*. New York: Macmillan.

Wright, P., McCarthy, J. (2008). Empathy and Experience in HCI. *CHI 2008*, April 5-10, 2008, Florence, Italy. pp. 637-646. DOI: 10.1145/1357054.1357156.

Wright, P., Wallace, J., McCarthy, J. (2008). Aesthetics and Experience-Centered Design. *ACM Transactions on Computer-Human Interaction (TOCHI)* Volume 15 Issue 4, November 2008. DOI: 10.1145/1460355.1460360.

Yoong, P. (1999). Making Sense of GSS Facilitation: A Reflective Practice Perspective. *Journal of Information Technology and People*, 12(1), 86-112. DOI: 10.1108/09593849910250565.

Yoong, P., Gallupe, R. (2002). Coherence in Face-to-Face Electronic Meetings: A Hidden Factor in Facilitation Success. *Group Facilitation: A Research and Applications Journal*. Issue #4 Summer 2002. Available online at http://www.iaf-world.org/i4a/pages/index.cfm?pageid=3502.

Zeiliger, R., Vermeulin, F., Esnault, L., Cherchem, N. (2008). Experiencing Pitfalls in the Participatory Design of Social Computing Services. *PDC '08: Proceedings of the Tenth Anniversary Conference on Participatory Design 2008*. New York: ACM Press. DOI: 10.1145/1795234.1795282.

Zorn, T. and Rosenfeld, L. (1989). Between a Rock and a Hard Place: Ethical Dilemmas in Problem-Solving Group Facilitation. *Management Communication Quarterly*, Vol. 3 No. 1, pp. 93-106.

Author Biographies

Albert M. Selvin (Al) is Director, User Experience, in the Information Technology organization at Verizon. His research interests lie in understanding how people engage in creating representations of complex problems. He was the original developer of the Compendium approach and software toolset at NYNEX Science & Technology in the early 1990s, and a member of its core design team at the Open University since 2000. As a practitioner, he has facilitated over 500 sessions for industry, academic, and community groups using the Compendium approach. Previously, he worked as a consultant, user interface designer, technical writer, researcher, and musician. He has traveled widely by bicycle and foot in Asia, Europe, and North America. He holds a B.A. in Film/Video Studies from the University of Michigan (1982), an M.A. in Communication Arts from the University of Wisconsin (1984), and a Ph.D. in Knowledge Media from The Open University, UK (2011). He resides in Dutchess County, New York with his family.

Simon J. Buckingham Shum is Professor of Learning Informatics at the University of Technology Sydney, where he is Director of the Connected Intelligence Centre. His research is at the intersection of sensemaking and computation: the invention of new digital tools and ways of thinking and working, that build the qualities needed for 21st-century learning. Specifically, he is interested in how computation can make the quality of thinking visible, to enable more reflective deliberation at a range of different scales from individuals, to small teams, to large networks. From 1995–2014 he was at The Open University's Knowledge Media Institute, which provided the academic environment for the projects underpinning this book. In his spare time he is a runner, and a kit and cajon drummer. He holds a B.Sc. in Psychology from the University of York (1987), an M.Sc. in Ergonomics from the University of London (1988) and a Ph.D. in Design Rationale from the University of York (1992). He lives with his family in Sydney.

Printed in the United States
by Baker & Taylor Publisher Services